# ECONOMIC FORECASTING

# ECONOMIC FORECASTING
## THE STATE OF THE ART

# ELIA KACAPYR

*M.E. Sharpe*
Armonk, New York
London, England

**Library of Congress Cataloging-in-Publication Data**

Kacapyr,
Elia, 1956–
Economic forecasting: the state of the art / Elia Kacapyr.
p.  cm.
Includes bibliographical references and index.
ISBN 1-56324-764-X (hardcover: alk. paper).
ISBN 1-56324-765-8 (pbk.: alk. paper)
1. Economic forecasting. I. Title.
HB3730.K2   1996
338.5′44—dc20
95-52008
CIP

Printed in the United States of America
The paper used in this publication meets the minimum
requirements of American National Standard for
Information Sciences—Permanence of Paper for
Printed Library Materials, ANSI Z 39.48-1984.


BM (c)   10   9   8   7   6   5   4   3   2   1
BM (p)   10   9   8   7   6   5   4   3   2   1

For

L
  L
   L

Forecasting occupies us all for much of our lives. It begins with the speculative wagging of heads over our cradles and continues until the prayers with which we are hopefully laid to rest. Sometimes it is an idle amusement, sometimes a matter of life and death, sometimes—and this is where the economist takes a hand—it carries rewards and punishments in the form of profit or loss.

—Sir Alec Cairncross, 1969

# Contents

# List of Tables

# List of Figures

# Preface

This book is written for those who study, use, and perhaps occasionally make, economic forecasts. It addresses the question of how forecasting is done. If you ever have been handed an ARIMA forecast or some exponentially smoothed data and wondered exactly what was done to obtain those numbers, this book will tell you.

This is a book on economic forecasting techniques. The focus is on macroeconomic forecasts, including forecasts of economic growth, interest rates, and employment for the entire economy. This distinguishes the book from others that concentrate on business forecasting, with an emphasis on predicting sales, prices, and inventories for a single firm or market. There is, however, some overlap between this book on economic forecasting and those concerned with business forecasting. Most important, some of the techniques explained here will work well in the setting of a single firm or market.

A perfectly detailed understanding of economic forecasting techniques requires a substantial background in mathematics and statistics. If you have that background, the notes at the end of each chapter and the bibliography at the end of the book will refer you to the major sources for each topic. If you do not have that background or do not wish to become involved with the fine details of each procedure, then this text will provide an intuitive understanding. In any case, the exposition here is intended to be as detailed as possible while remaining accessible to the typical businessperson.

Another objective of this book is to answer the question Which forecasting technique works best? For GDP? For interest rates? For the long, short, or intermediate term? These questions are answered along the way, and formally in the last chapter.

The first chapter gives an overview of the economic forecasting industry in the United States. The second chapter discusses the business cycle—the nonperiodic but recurrent ups and downs in economic activity that make forecasting such a difficult endeavor. Theories about long waves in economic activity are taken up in the third chapter. Chapters four through seven present the forecasting techniques.

Throughout the presentation, every attempt is made to be plainspoken. Nevertheless, the good reader will become acquainted with the dominant jargon of the forecasting profession. You will certainly understand the basics of ARIMA forecasting and exponential smoothing (chapter 5) and the handful of other techniques that comprise the state of the art in economic forecasting.

# ECONOMIC FORECASTING

# Introduction to Economic Forecasting

Despite our years of learning and our efforts at education, we still find
our patients and clients longing for relief and turning, with distressing
frequency, to today's equivalent of snake oil and witchcraft.

—Paul Volker, 1993

There is nothing novel about making economic projections. By 1930,
Garfield Cox's book, *An Appraisal of American Business Forecasts,*
was in its second edition. Almost seventy years later Cox's title is still
apt. Before 1940, however, there was no distinction between "business" forecasts and "economic" forecasts. Even today, some professionals see no need to differentiate between the two. Yet almost
everyone in the field understands that business forecasting primarily
appertains to predictions about the performance of individual firms or
industries. Economic forecasting, on the other hand, is associated with
making predictions about the economy of a region or of the entire
nation. The distinction between the two types of forecasting is not
crisp because they share some of the same techniques. One often finds
the same persons and establishments practicing in both fields.

To complicate matters further, there is much discussion about the
*business* cycle—the ups and downs in overall economic activity. The
term "business cycle," however, is a throwback to before World War
II. To conform with the distinction between business and economic
forecasting, the term "economic cycle" would be more appropriate
than "business" cycle. The traditional terminology is too ingrained to
change.

This book concentrates on economic forecasting. How do forecasters produce predictions about interest rates, employment, prices, production levels, and the like? What are the intricacies involved in these sorts of projections and how accurate are they? In short, the reader will be introduced to the art of economic forecasting.

## The Value of Economic Forecasts

Some skeptics would assert that economic forecasts are of very little value. Consider the epigram from the noted economist John Kenneth Galbraith: "We have two sorts of forecasters: Those who don't know—and those who don't know they don't know." It is impossible to deny the bravado of economic forecasters, but it would be unfair to call them cavalier. Most are keenly aware of the precariousness of their prognostications. It is just that these forecasters are not discouraged by the difficulty of the task at hand.

And there is much that is discouraging. For instance, turning points in economic activity—the transition periods from positive to negative growth, or vice versa—give forecasters fits. Take the brief but severe recession that began in January 1980. The forecasting consensus did not see the contraction coming. And when they finally did predict declines in economic growth, they vastly underestimated the magnitude of the decline.

In another case, thirty-five out of forty economists surveyed by *The Wall Street Journal* in mid-1990 foresaw no recession in the next twelve months. The recession began the very next month.

Forecasters do slightly better in spotting the transition from recession to expansion. This is easier to do because recessions have much narrower time spans than do expansions. An expansion may last anywhere from one to more than ten years. Contractions, on the other hand, rarely last more than one year. For this reason, as soon as it is established that a recession is in progress, it is safe to start predicting its demise.

Aside from turning points, another problem area for forecasters is interest rates. *The Wall Street Journal* has been polling economists with respect to interest rates semiannually since 1981. That particular forecasting record has been abysmally poor. Economists do much better when it comes to predicting inflation rates. This is remarkable because, theoretically, interest rates and inflation rates are highly correlated.

Economic forecasters have registered many more successes than they have failures. The botched forecasts are only remembered because of selective retention. If one goes fishing and comes home with the expected catch, there is nothing much to tell. But if one catches nothing or an exorbitant amount, then we have a story, not only to tell, but to remember. The forecasting triumphs, however, hardly ever involve turning points or interest rates.

In the final chapter of this book we methodically investigate the economic forecasting record. One of the things that will come to light from this inquiry is that economists are fairly accurate when it comes to predicting rates of economic growth, inflation, and unemployment. Interest rates, especially long-term interest rates, are predicted with less acumen.

But the focus on accuracy is misplaced in a discussion of the value of economic forecasts. The forecasts are useful if they reduce uncertainty and lead to better decisions. And the usefulness of economic forecasts cannot be denied. The strongest evidence of this is the rise of the forecasting industry. Today, billions of dollars' worth of economic forecasts are purchased in private markets. This does not include the forecasts provided by government agencies and not-for-profit academic establishments. It is absurd to think that all of the forecasts that are demanded and paid for, in actuality, have no merit. Shrewd businesspersons simply do not make those kinds of mistakes consistently.

For politicians, economists, businesspersons, and others concerned with the state of the economy, forecasts help shape the debate over economic policy. Should the growth rate of the money supply be raised? By exactly how much? Are tax cuts feasible at this point in time? How many jobs would be lost if federal spending were reduced by $25 billion? It makes sense to address questions such as these with estimates of their effects on various facets of the economy. The estimates may vary widely, and none of them may be correct, yet the exercise of developing them will be instructive. The forecasting process can highlight one's assumptions about the way the economy works. Be prepared to defend these assumptions in the policy debate.

As an example of this sort of benefit from economic forecasting, consider what would happen if the federal government were able to curb its deficit spending to some degree. One effect of this policy would be lower interest rates. Interest rates would fall because the

Table 1.1

**Thirty-Year Treasury Bond Yield Forecasts**

If the federal deficit is permanently reduced, the yield on thirty-year Treasury bonds, now 7.3%, would eventually decline to:

| Estimate by | After a cut of $\100 bil. | After a cut of $200 bil. |
| --- | --- | --- |
| The Boston Co. | 6.60% | 5.91% |
| Data Resources Inc. | 6.40% | 5.75% |
| WEFA Group | 6.40% | 5.90% |

*Source: The Wall Street Journal,* January 25, 1993, p. C1.

government would not be required to borrow as much to cover its spending. Since the federal government is not demanding as much of the loanable funds available, more funds are left for private borrowers. And, therefore, private borrowers should be able to obtain loans at lower interest rates.

All this sounds logical, but is this the way the economy works? Yes—at least according to three economic forecasting establishments: *The Wall Street Journal* asked three leading forecasting firms to provide estimates of long-term interest rates if the government reduced the deficit by $100 billion and $200 billion, respectively. The forecasts are found in Table 1.1.

It is not surprising that all three firms came up with similar forecasts. They all relied primarily on the same technique—an econometric model of the economy.[1] It must be that all three of their models have the deficit-reduction/interest-rate-reduction theory built into them.

One of the most important functions of economic forecasts is to provide predictions such as these. We may now argue about whether it is correct to assume that interest rates will fall if the federal deficit is reduced. If we agree that the assumption is sound, then we can decide whether the benefits from reduced rates are worth the pain caused by reducing deficits (which can only occur through spending cuts or revenue increases). The point is that economic forecasts help to shape economic policy and lead to better policy decisions.

In a similar fashion, economic forecasts can aid individual households or firms in making better, more confident decisions. Imagine a household that is thinking about refinancing the mortgage on their home. Should they refinance now or wait till rates fall still further? Will rates continue to fall? By how much in the next six months? The same questions would be asked by the chief financial officer of a firm contemplating paying down some of its debt. Some households, and even some business establishments, fly by the seat of their pants when they confront decisions such as these. But the risk of their responses can be minimized by consulting the financial media for the latest consensus forecast or by subscribing to one of the forecasting services.

## Pitfalls and Pointers

The field of economic forecasting is fraught with pitfalls. We have already encountered two: turning points and long-term interest rates. This section points out some of the other problem areas for forecasters.

### The Business Cycle

It is well established that economic growth proceeds in fits and starts. Since 1960 the average annual growth rate of economic activity in the United States has been 3 percent. But the economy has grown by this average in only five of those years. The fact that economic progress is not uniform greatly hampers forecasting.

Not only do rates of growth fluctuate, but so do the other fundamental features of the business cycle. For instance, economic boom times—expansions—vary greatly in length. In the postwar era, the shortest expansion lasted twelve months (July 1980-July 1981) while the longest was 106 months (February 1961-December 1969). The length of recessionary periods has varied between six and sixteen months.

The next chapter will investigate the principal features of business cycles in detail. If the phenomenon is better understood, it may be easier to predict. For now, the point is that the variegated nature of the business cycle is a major obstacle to accurate and effective economic forecasting.

### Economic Data

Most economic forecasters are data experts—not by choice, but through necessity. Mundane details about economic data are crucial information to forecasters. What is the Commerce Department's release date for such and such a figure? When are the revisions available? Are the revisions usually significant? Should seasonally adjusted data be considered or not? What about adjustments for inflation?

And it is always important to consider the components of each figure. The latest release may show the economy growing at a healthy clip. But if a large portion of the gains can be attributed to inventory accumulation, then the situation is more troublesome.

The vast array of statistics available and their particulars can beguile the nonexpert. Take the case of the employment figures in the middle of 1994.[2] From April to May the unemployment rate fell substantially to 6.0 percent from 6.4 percent. Good news, except to forecasters who did not see the substantial decline coming. But the bad news was that the number of jobs created in May was just 191,000—far too little to account for the hefty drop in unemployment.

What did account for the drop in the unemployment rate? One possibility is that a lot of persons quit the labor force. If people retire or just stop looking for work, they are not considered unemployed. They are not part of the labor force. So if a lot of people retired in May or gave up looking for work, then the unemployment rate could have fallen to 6.0 percent despite the small number of jobs created.

A more likely explanation is that the separate surveys used to come up with each figure erred in opposite directions. The unemployment figure is derived from a survey of households, while the estimate of the number of jobs created comes from a survey of employers.

Situations where the figures give conflicting signals, as did the employment numbers in 1994, are common with economic statistics. This explains why it is possible to find economists to support just about any position on a given issue. It also explains how it is possible for politicians to rattle off a host of statistics to advance their view, regardless of what that view might be. The fact that it is possible to slant virtually any statistic is what gave rise to the maxim, "Liars, damn liars, and statisticians!" The wide assortment of economic numbers just makes the slanting easier to accomplish in this particular field.

Imagine, however, the dilemma of an economic forecaster in mid-1994 who is trying to make an unbiased assessment of the employment picture. Is it improving dramatically as the unemployment rate suggests, or moderately as the number of new jobs would have it? The answer, as often occurs in situations like these, is in the middle. Months later, May's unemployment rate would be revised upward to

6.1 percent from 6.0 percent and the number of new jobs created would be revised to 252,000 from 191,000. Those revisions, however, were of no help to forecasters who had to make predictions based on the data available at that particular time.

Stories such as this make it apparent that economic data, despite the enormous and largely successful effort put into gathering them, present several pitfalls to the forecaster. The most crucial thing to know about economic statistics, more important than their timeliness or reliability, is exactly what is being measured and how it is being measured.

Again, consider the unemployment rate. It is important to understand that it is estimated from a survey of 60,000 families each month. One of the questions that the Bureau of Labor Statistics asks in its survey concerns whether the respondent has been looking for work recently. If the answer is no, then the person is not considered to be in the labor force and is not, therefore, unemployed. This results in an unemployment statistic that understates the "true" amount of unemployment because it does not count those persons who are too discouraged to look for work.

Moreover, if a person is working in a part-time job, but would like to work full-time, he or she is counted as if he were fully employed. Because of this, the official unemployment rate will understate the severity of the unemployment problem. On the other hand, some people may state that they have been looking for work when in reality they have not, or that they are unemployed when they have an "under-the-table" job. These factors cause the official unemployment rate to overestimate the "true" rate.

Another statistic that is important for the reader to understand, since it is used extensively throughout this book, is gross domestic product (GDP). GDP represents the dollar value of all the goods and services produced. The Department of Commerce estimates this amount quarterly. One may well ask, "How do they know?" They have a small army of people working on it. Each soldier is responsible for estimating the production of one product or group of products. They take surveys and stay in touch with the major manufacturers and retailers to distill their numbers. For 1994 GDP was $6.7 trillion.

This amount, $6.7 trillion, is a gross underestimate of all that was produced in the United States in 1994. There are many things that the Department of Commerce does not even try to count. For instance, if you repair your own car the value of that service is not counted in

GDP. Any good or service that you provide yourself instead of purchasing is not counted or estimated in any way in the official estimate of GDP. Thus, if you marry your auto mechanic, you will lower official GDP.

Now consider all the illegal drugs and gambling produced and distributed in this country each year. Estimates of illicit activities such as these are not included in official GDP either. Both the innocent do-it-yourself production and the pernicious activities, such as illegal gambling, are part of the "underground" economy. Estimates of the size of the underground economy range anywhere from 5 percent to 25 percent of the official economy. Thus, actual production in 1994 is closer to $8 trillion than to $6.7 trillion.

At least the Department of Commerce is consistent in its estimating procedures for GDP. It has *never* counted the underground economy. Consequently, it is fair to compare the $6.7 trillion figure for 1994 with that of $6.3 trillion for 1993. Still, one cannot conclude from these figures that more was produced in 1994 than in 1993. This is because the prices of the products may have increased from 1993 to 1994 while their production levels held steady or even declined. To determine just what happened to production levels, the GDP figures have to be adjusted for price changes.

Adjusting GDP for price changes is easily accomplished. Take the prices from some year in the past—it does not matter which year—and apply them to the production levels from this year. The resulting statistic is known as *real* GDP. This terminology can be generalized for all economic statistics: the word "real" before any statistic implies that it has been adjusted for price changes.

Thus, real GDP in 1993 is 1993 production valued at prices from some base year in the past—say, 1987. Real GDP in 1994 is 1994 production valued at 1987 prices. If real GDP is higher in 1994 than in 1993, and it was—$5.3 trillion to $5.1 trillion—then it must be because more was produced. It could not have been higher prices because prices are held constant at 1987 levels for the calculation of real GDP.

Real GDP is the premier statistic for monitoring the economy's progress. Before 1992, real gross *national* product (GNP) was the foremost statistic for measuring economic growth. The Department of Commerce switched to emphasizing real GDP primarily to conform with the growth measures from other nations. For the United States, GDP and GNP are not much different in magnitude. The difference lies in how foreign nationals are treated. Consider an American citizen working in Japan for a U.S. multinational bank. Should the services produced by this person be counted in U.S. production? They are counted in the GNP of the United States; since a U.S. citizen is producing financial services, it does not matter where those services are produced. The financial services produced by the U.S. citizen in Japan are not, however, counted in U.S. GDP. GDP counts only domestic production. So the things produced by foreigners working in the United States are counted in our GDP, but not our GNP.

In any event, both GDP and GNP are used throughout this book. Before 1992, the major forecasting establishments were providing forecasts of GNP only. Any examination of the forecasting record that goes back before 1992 will require digging out the old GNP figures because that is what was being predicted.

If you find all these details about economic statistics boring, join the club. But keeping up with data revisions and understanding exactly how a particular statistic is derived are pointers toward good forecasting.

### Sources of Forecast Errors

As we saw in the previous section, the data themselves are a source of forecast errors. The large revisions, several months later, in the May employment figures handicapped the forecasts that were based on the unrevised data. But there are other pitfalls to accurate predictions for the macroeconomy.

Perhaps the most fundamental, and frustrating, source of forecast errors is unforeseen events that impact the economy. A sudden unanticipated military conflict, such as Desert Storm, is an example. The economic lingo for such phenomena is "exogenous shock." There are wars, natural disasters, labor strikes, and unanticipated changes in economic policy, both domestic and foreign. The largest of these external shocks in the postwar era was the OPEC oil embargo in the early 1970s. That shock was largely responsible for a sixteen-month recession and a severe bout of inflation.

The simultaneous occurrence of both economic bogeymen in 1973 was a new experience for the pundits, most of whom believed it to be theoretically impossible. As one can imagine, forecasters were thrown for a loop. This leads us to another source of poor forecasts—faulty theory. We shall see in chapter 6 that the predominant forecasting technique in use today relies on mathematical specifications of economic relationships. These mathematical models of the economy have no hope of generating accurate forecasts if they do not specify correctly the relations among economic variables. In other words, forecasts need to be based on proper theory.

But this is easier said than accomplished. In the early 1970s, most economic models, and most economists for that matter, had embedded in them a theory known as the *Phillips trade-off*. This theory stipulated that times of high inflation would be associated with low levels of unemployment and vice versa. The theory worked perfectly fine for over a hundred years. Professor Phillips' original paper, published in 1958, investigated the relationship between inflation and unemployment back to 1861 in the United Kingdom.[3] The theory became unsuitable when the economic landscape changed dramatically in 1973. In that year, and for several to follow, the OPEC oil cartel created a climate where high prices could coexist with high unemployment. It is not that economic theory was wrong, it simply became outmoded. The economic environment had changed and the relationships that were valid in the old order were no longer reliable.

The ever-changing structure of the economy alters economic relationships and thereby hinders forecasts based on those connections. Forecasters must be vigilant to ensure that theory fits reality. To the extent that forecasters meet this challenge, they provide a benefit to the theoretical side of the field of economics.

A change in the economic panorama can come from a variety of sources, not just an oil cartel. One of the most conventional sources is Washington, D.C. Changes in government spending, taxes, and other policies can upset economic relationships and foil predictions. A recurrent source of forecast errors is policy changes.

This can give rise to a circular link between economic forecasts and economic policy. As mentioned above, forecasts help forge the policy debate and therefore the policy itself. Now we are saying that the policy can affect the forecast, or at least cause the forecast to be errant. In frustration, some forecasters have claimed that their predictions have no hope of coming to fruition since policy makers take offsetting actions once they get wind of the forecast. Others believe that this is giving too much credit to the competence of policy makers. On the other hand, there is a whole school of economic thought based on the premise that economic policy will be ineffective unless the policy change is unanticipated. If the policy change is anticipated (forecasted), then countervailing actions will be taken by economic agents.[4] Regardless of one's beliefs in these matters, it must be admitted that economic policy can be a sort of exogenous shock that results in erroneous forecasts.

Another possible source of forecast error is the forecasting technique itself. Each forecasting technique has its own strengths and deficiencies. As we just saw, mathematical models have a tendency to cling to defunct theories as the economy's structure evolves. Vector autoregressions (discussed at the end of chapter 6) attempt to avoid this problem by assuming that everything is related to everything. That assumption, however, does not preclude the possibility that the way in which something is related to everything else may change through time.

Other techniques have their own detriments. Time-series techniques, examined in chapter 5, do not rely on economic theory. These techniques uncover patterns and extrapolate them into the future. Time-series methods are impressive in their ability to discover patterns that are not readily apparent in the past behavior of economic variables. But there is no guarantee that the patterns will hold in the future.

Economic indicators, statistics that change direction before the overall economy, are a customary method of fabricating predictions about the business cycle. The strong and weak points of this technique are taken up in chapter 4. One of the weak points is the tendency of economic indicators to cry wolf when no change is imminent. Figure 1.1 shows the precipitous nine-month decline in the index of leading economic indicators that occurred in late 1966. Notice that economic growth, as measured by real GDP, continued unabated.

In chapter 7 the value obtained from combining forecasts from several techniques or sources is appraised. The consensus forecast can mask some of the deficiencies of the individual forecasts that comprise it. By definition, however, the consensus forecast of, say, real GDP growth in 1998, can never be more accurate than the best individual forecast. The trouble is that it is very difficult to pick which individual forecast or method will be most accurate at any particular time.

**The Art of Forecasting**

Because some forecasting techniques are better in certain situations than others, because of the numerous pitfalls, and because there is no

Figure 1.1 **Leading Economic Indicators and Real GDP** (1965–69)

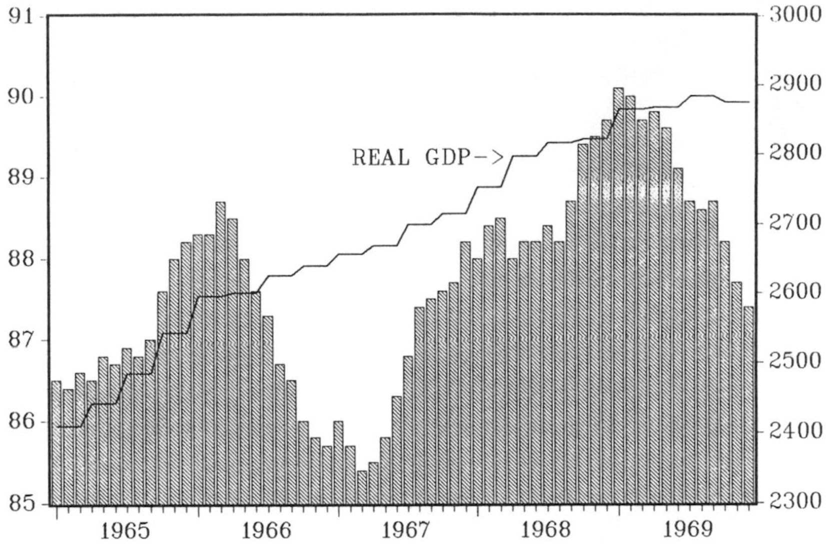

set way of handling these hazards, economic forecasting is an art. This is not to deny that there are scientific elements to the discipline. The statistical theory behind regression analysis, which we touch upon in chapter 6, is pure science. In fact, all the tools of the forecasting trade—autoregressive models, econometric models, vector autoregressions, diffusion indexes, and other statistical indicators—have very little, if any, artistic aspects per se. It is the manner in which these tools are employed and the fact that the results derived from them are adjusted to conform with the inclinations of the forecaster that lend a quality of craft to the endeavor.

There is no universally optimal method for blending all of the ingredients for an economic forecast. Even if we ignore all the concerns about data reliability and revisions, all the questions over the impact of recent policy changes, and all the speculation over possible exogenous shocks to the economy, there still remains the question about which basic forecasting technique is best. In chapter 8 we shall see that no forecasting procedure or establishment is pervasively superior. Some techniques, and some forecasters, have a history of performing well for a given variable over a particular time horizon. But these track records may not hold in the future. Nevertheless, the astute forecast user, like the crafty bettor at the racetrack, knows the inside line.

Table 1.2

**Letter Grades Given to Various Fields in Forecasting**

| Field | Forecasting Ability |
| --- | --- |
| Quantum mechanics | A |
| Celestial mechanics | A |
| Weather | A− |
| Chemistry | B+ |
| Mathematics | B |
| Stock market | C+ |
| Climate | C |
| War | C− |
| Developmental biology | D+ |
| Economics | D |
| Evolutionary biology | D− |

*Source*: Casti (1990), p. 407.

In his book *Searching for Certainty: What Scientists Can Know about the Future,* John Casti (1990) gives economic forecasters poor grades. In fact, economists were ranked dead last not only in capability to predict, but also in ability to analyze and explain economic changes. Biologists, chemists, physicists, astronomers, meteorologists, and even stock market analysts were judged to be more competent than the lowly economists (see Table 1.2).

This book does not dispute Professor Casti's ordering. It should be pointed out, however, that the ranking would look quite different if the forecasters had been handicapped according to degree of difficulty. The pages that follow are a testament to the perspicacity of economic forecasters.

**Summary**

The value of economic forecasts is evident in the ascension of the forecasting industry. Economic forecasts are in demand because they lead to better decisions by businesspersons, administrators, policy makers, and households. Moreover, forecasts help to formulate the important economic questions facing us all. It is difficult to make a good forecast without an understanding of the underlying economic forces. In this manner, economic forecasting facilitates the refinement of economic theory.

Despite its scientific aspects, the forecasting profession incorporates a good share of craft or art, if you will. The uncertainties caused by impaired data, exogenous shocks to the economy, and changes in the economic structure give rise to the "artistic" aspects of the discipline. The difficulties posed by these impediments have made forecasting more challenging in economics than in other fields.

## Notes

1. This technique is explained in chapter 6.
2. The details of this story were presented in a June 5, 1994 *New York Times* article by Floyd Norris.
3. See Phillips (1958).
4. I am certain that rational expectations theorists will howl at this unfairly terse description of their school. The foundations of rational expectations go back to Muth (1961). The school took shape in the mid-1970s with articles such as Sargent and Wallace (1975). For an assessment of the rational expectations school, see Begg (1982).

## References

Begg, David K. 1982. *The Rational Expectations Revolution in Macroeconomics: Theories and Evidence.* Baltimore: Johns Hopkins University Press.

Casti, John L. 1990. *Searching for Certainty.* New York: Morrow.

Cox, Garfield. 1930. *An Appraisal of American Business Forecasts,* 2d ed. Chicago: University of Chicago Press.

Muth, John F. 1961. "Rational Expectations and the Theory of Price Movements." *Econometrica* (July): 315–35.

Phillips, A.W. 1958. "The Relationship between Unemployment and the Rate of Change of Money Wage Rates in the United Kingdom: 1861–1957." *Economica,* 25: 283–99.

Sargent, Thomas J., and Neil Wallace. 1975. "Rational Expectations, the Optimal Monetary Instrument, and the Optimal Money Supply Rule." *Journal of Political Economy* (April): 241–57.

# 2

# Business Cycles

The inevitable never happens. It is the unexpected always.

—John Maynard Keynes, 1927

Modern economies do not advance at constant growth rates. Economies experience fits and starts as they move toward the distant and
unknown future. Booms and busts are thought to be an inherent characteristic of capitalistic economies, and there is ample evidence that socialist
economies also experience business cycles.[1] For a time in the 1960s in the
United States, economists spoke of the demise of economic fluctuations.
These discussions, as it turns out, were unwarranted.

### The Three D's of Business Cycles

Textbooks often employ a diagram such as Figure 2.1 to illustrate the
phases of the business cycle: the peak, the trough, the contraction, the
expansion. The problem is that this diagram makes business cycles
seem uniform. If there is one thing economists are certain about, it is
that these cycles are not uniform. If only they were, economic forecasting would be a simple matter.

Figure 2.2 shows the actual business cycles in the United States
since World War II. Specifically, the chart depicts the growth rate of
real GDP. The vertical lines indicate recessions. Clearly, uniformity is
lacking.

Changes in economic activity, by their nature, are difficult to predict. The term "business cycle" is deceptive because the ups and
downs of the aggregate economy are not uniform in any respect. If the

Figure 2.1 **Hypothetical Business Cycles**

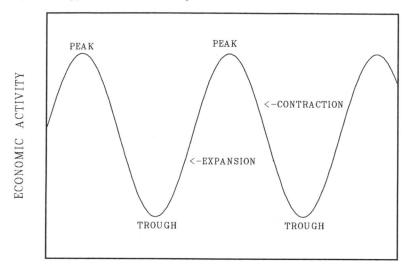

YEARS

cycles were periodic, forecasting turning points in economic activity would be an uncomplicated task. In fact, business cycles differ not only in their duration, but also in their depth and dispersion—the "three D's" of business cycles. Each cycle is unique with respect to these characteristics.

## Duration

In the postwar United States, the average length of an expansion is fifty months. Any given expansion, however, can diverge widely from this average. The 1980–81 expansion lasted only twelve months, while the 1961–69 expansion lasted almost nine years. The average duration of contractions in the postwar period is substantially smaller than that of the expansions—just under eleven months. But again, there can be significant deviation from this average. The shortest postwar contraction was just six months in length (from January to July of 1980), while the longest was sixteen months (two recessions lasted sixteen months—1973–75 and 1981–82). Thus, it would entail extreme naivete to predict the end of an expansion or a recession simply because it approached or surpassed the average duration.

Figure 2.2 **Actual Business Cycles in the United States** (percentage change in real GDP)

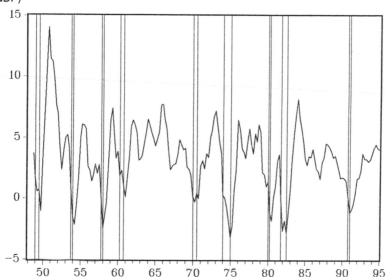

A complete business cycle is comprised of an expansion and a recession. There is no convention as to which comes first, the expansion or the recession. In analytical terms, it makes no difference if the cycle is defined as an expansion followed by a recession, or the other way around. The average length of an entire cycle is, however, affected by which phase is considered the initial one. It would be fifty-six months if the recovery period comes first and sixty-one months if the contraction is considered the initial stage.

With all the data, much of which is contradictory, churned out concerning the national economy, one may wonder how the exact dates of recessions and revivals are determined. Basically, an umpire is needed to make the call and that umpire is the Business Cycle Dating Committee of the National Bureau of Economic Research (NBER). This committee, composed of well-respected economists, considers the evidence in order to come to some sort of consensus about the exact month that a particular recovery or recession began. A variety of evidence is considered, but, for the most part, a plethora of data is scrutinized to determine exactly when the economy as a whole experienced a turning point. The phrase "as a whole" is crucial and renders the dating of turning points somewhat subjective. The data considered by the NBER Committee do not, unfortunately, all turn around on the same month.

Figure 2.3 **The 1990–91 Recession**

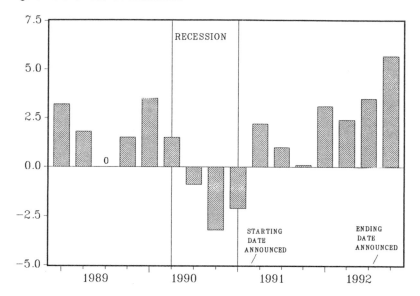

Thus, a recovery may be declared to begin in a particular month even though the unemployment rate is still rising. In fact, it is typical for the unemployment rate to increase during the initial months of expansions, as demarcated by the NBER Dating Committee.

A whole host of sometimes contradictory data must be considered and reconciled with other evidence, such as current events and economic policy. Because of the time lag involved in acquiring and compiling the data (not to mention data revisions), and the sense of perspective needed to cite a definite turning point, starting dates are not declared by the NBER Committee until well after the fact. As Figure 2.3 shows, the recession that was declared to have commenced in July 1990 was not announced until April 1991, at which point the recession was already over; it had ended the previous month (according to an NBER press release in December 1992!).

Obviously, the NBER Dating Committee wants to be certain of these dates and does not want to have to retract or revise them. The time lag this involves says something about the precariousness of macroeconomic forecasting: If well-respected economists, armed with the most recent data available, cannot be certain that a recession has begun until after it has ended, what chance does anyone have of forecasting the onset of a recession in advance of its occurrence?

There are other measures of the duration of business cycles besides those of the NBER Dating Committee. One frequently used rule is to declare the beginning of a recession when GDP growth (adjusted for inflation) becomes negative and remains negative for at least two quarters. This definition can also result in untimely identification of turning points in the cycle because of data lags and revisions. The dates it produces tend to differ slightly from those promulgated by the NBER, although exact comparisons cannot be made since the GDP data are quarterly, whereas the NBER designates a specific month as the turning point.

### Depth

A second characteristic of business cycles is their severity, or depth. When a contraction is severe, it may be referred to as a "depression," as opposed to the usual "recession."[2] The last contraction to merit this distinction was the Great Depression, which, according to the NBER Dating Committee, began in August 1929. The unemployment rate reached 24.9 percent during the Great Depression, while industrial production plummeted 53.4 percent.

There is no terminological distinction between a typical expansion and those that are more exuberant, although the term "boom" is sometimes used in this manner.

Although the severity of recessions and the exuberance of revivals can be measured in various ways, the percentage change in real GDP is the predominant method. GDP is a measure of overall economic activity. Because of the manner in which it is constructed, GDP approximates not only production in the economy, but total income and total spending as well. Thus, it is a good measure of overall economic performance.[3] The U.S. Department of Commerce reports an advance estimate of GDP quarterly with a time lag of one month. Although the advance, or "flash" estimate of GDP is regarded seriously, especially by the financial markets, it can be subject to substantial revision. There are two standard revisions which come two and three months after the end of the quarter under consideration. These are known as the preliminary and final estimates, although the latter is by no means final. Further standard revisions come one, two, three, and five years later. And there can be other, unexpected revisions.

The average annual growth rate of real GDP has been about 3

percent in the postwar period. But, because of the business cycle, one is hard-pressed to find a year when real GDP grew by its average. When GDP is growing, but by less than its average, this is sometimes referred to as a "growth recession." A genuine recession is accompanied by negative real GDP growth rates. Some textbooks define a recession as at least two consecutive quarters of negative real GDP growth. As indicated earlier, the NBER Dating Committee uses no such rule.

There are alternative measures of the depth of expansions and contractions. The most common alternatives are:

- the maximum (or minimum, in the case of expansions) unemployment rate attained;
- the change in the unemployment rate during the episode;
- the percentage change in industrial production;
- the change in the number of persons employed;
- the difference between actual and potential GDP.

The various measures of depth are not always complementary. Indeed, if each measure was used to rank the depth of recessions and expansions in the postwar economy, the ranking would be slightly different in each case. Nevertheless, the various measures usually concur and allow for robust estimation of the depth of business cycles (see Gordon, 1986, p. 542).

### Dispersion

Another distinguishing characteristic of business cycles is their dispersion. Recessions and expansions can affect a broad range of industries throughout the entire economy, or they can be concentrated on only a few. The 1969–70 recession was thought to have its biggest impact on the financial sector of the economy, leaving industrial production relatively unscathed. The 1948–49 recession, on the other hand, was well dispersed, with 90 percent of the industries in the economy experiencing declines in employment.

The percentage of industries experiencing declines, or increases, in employment is the predominant method for measuring the dispersion of contractions, or expansions. Again, alternative measures are available. The alternative measures of dispersion track a variety of eco-

Table 2.1

**Duration, Depth, and Dispersion of Postwar Recessions and Expansions**

Recessions

| Date | Duration (months) | Depth | Dispersion |
|------|-------------------|-------|------------|
| Nov. 48–Oct. 49 | 11 | −3.3 | n.a. |
| Jul. 53–May 54 | 10 | −3.9 | n.a. |
| Aug. 57–Apr. 58 | 8 | −8.5 | n.a. |
| Mar. 60–Feb. 61 | 10 | −2.5 | n.a. |
| Dec. 69–Nov. 70 | 11 | −3.0 | n.a. |
| Nov. 73–Mar. 75 | 16 | −8.7 | n.a. |
| Jan. 80–Jul. 80 | 6 | −9.9 | 62.9 |
| Jul. 81–Nov. 82 | 16 | −6.2 | 71.5 |
| Jul. 90–Mar. 91 | 8 | −3.2 | 69.8 |

Depth is measured by the *minimum* annualized quarterly growth rate of real GDP during the recession. Dispersion is measured by the percentage of industries experiencing declining employment (highest monthly reading).

Expansions

| Date | Duration (months) | Depth | Dispersion |
|------|-------------------|-------|------------|
| Oct. 45–Nov. 48 | 37 | 18.3 | n.a. |
| Oct. 49–Jul. 53 | 45 | 15.9 | n.a. |
| May 54–Aug. 57 | 39 | 10.8 | n.a. |
| Apr. 58–Apr. 60 | 24 | 9.0 | n.a. |
| Feb. 61–Dec. 69 | 106 | 10.4 | n.a. |
| Nov. 70–Nov. 73 | 36 | 10.2 | n.a. |
| Mar. 75–Jan. 80 | 58 | 13.5 | 81.8 |
| Jul. 80–Jul. 81 | 12 | 8.3 | 70.9 |
| Nov. 82–Jul. 90 | 92 | 11.3 | 80.2 |

Depth is measured by the *maximum* annualized growth rate of real GDP during the expansion. Dispersion is measured by the percentage of industries experiencing employment growth (highest monthly reading).

*Source:* U.S. Department of Commerce.

nomic statistics and score them according to whether they are rising, falling, or holding steady. Such statistics are commonly referred to as "diffusion" indexes. The diffusion indexes of the Commerce Department are the best known (these are discussed in chapter 4 since they are fundamental tools in economic forecasting).

Table 2.1 shows the "three D's" of business cycles in the United States since World War II.

### *Other Characteristics*

Business cycles can, and usually do, differ with regard to their duration, depth, and dispersion. This, of course, greatly hinders accurate forecasting. One's first impulse is to look for patterns, but the variegated nature of the business cycle obscures them, if, indeed, there are any. Some patterns have been identified and referred to as "waves" or "cycles" by their adherents. These are taken up and evaluated in the next chapter. At this point, it is tempting to entertain the notion that business cycles are random in their characteristics, but that simply is not true. If economic activity were truly random, there would be no business "cycle" to speak of at all.

But there is a cycle—pronounced periods of recession and recovery that tend to exhibit similarities. For instance, contractions are typically shorter than expansions. The beginning of an expansion is usually more vigorous than the later stages. Another point that is often asserted and used for forecasting is that a deep contraction is usually followed by a brisk recovery, and, conversely, a mild recession is followed by a weak recovery.[4] Further characteristics of the business cycle involve the manner in which certain components of the aggregate economy behave over the course of the cycle.[5] For example, there is less pressure on prices to rise during a contraction, more during a recovery.[6] Business spending on plant and equipment is observed to fluctuate more sharply over the course of the cycle than other forms of spending—usually. Interest rates tend to fall, or at least rise less rapidly, during contractions—but not always.[7]

Volumes have been written examining the behavior of various facets of the macroeconomy over the business cycle.[8] The money supply, the stock market, labor productivity, personal savings—all exhibit some sort of cyclical behavior. Some of these data series have been found to swing up or down before overall economic activity. The most dependable of these have been codified into the well-known leading indicator series of the Department of Commerce. Their use in forecasting is obvious, but their actual value and track record are a matter of contention and are discussed in detail in chapter 4. For now, we should note that, although many aspects of the economy display cyclical behavior, caveats like "usually" and "but not always" imply that there are no hard and fast rules concerning business cycles.

### Are Modern Business Cycles Different?

Before we turn to a review of the theoretical explanations for the existence of business cycles, it is instructive to investigate another often noted feature of these cycles. It has been observed that expansions have become longer and contractions have become shorter, and both have become less severe since World War II.[9] A variety of explanations have been put forth regarding this phenomenon. Reviewing them will give some idea of the large number of factors that can, at any time, impinge upon the business-cycle process.

#### *Automatic Stabilizers*

The reduced severity of business cycles in the postwar era has been attributed to "automatic," or "built-in" stabilizers. The most important automatic stabilizers in the U.S. economy are personal and corporate income taxes, unemployment compensation, and other "welfare" programs. For example, if we look at a case where the economy is experiencing a slow-down, a decrease in tax collections or an increase in government spending would help bolster incomes and, therefore, spending and production.

Legislation is already in place to provide for this. Since the personal and corporate income taxes are based on the level of income and profits, the government will automatically experience reduced revenues from these sources during a contraction. Moreover, government spending on unemployment compensation, food stamps, and aid to families with dependent children (AFDC) will increase as more individuals become eligible for these payments during the downturn in economic activity.

Thus, built-in stabilizers can ameliorate the severity of a cyclical contraction, but cannot prevent them outright. This is because declines in income and production are necessary to invoke the stabilizers in the first place. Automatic stabilizers also can work to prevent expansions from becoming overly exuberant. As the economy heats up, incomes climb and production strains its capacity. Government tax collections automatically increase, and government spending on income-maintenance programs decreases, perhaps defusing an inflationary situation.[10]

The advantage of built-in stabilizers is that, since the laws are already in place and function automatically, they require no invocation by the government or new legislation. If we keep this in mind, the diminished severity of business cycles can be attributed to the increased prominence of automatic stabilizers since World War II. True, the personal income tax was initiated in 1913, but it was a mere 1 percent on most income earners. Government spending on welfare programs became more commonplace after the Great Depression. Yet, it was not until after 1945 that income-maintenance programs became dominant enough to mitigate against the severity of cyclical fluctuations.

Automatic stabilizers cannot make the economy recession-proof or inflation-proof, but they can make the economy depression-proof and hyperinflation-proof.

### *Fiscal Policy*

Another explanation for the diminished amplitude of economic fluctuations in the postwar era is the federal government's increased adroitness at implementing fiscal policy. Before Keynes—indeed, before World War II—deficit spending was generally considered imprudent. The gradual, though still incomplete, acceptance of fiscal policy as a stabilization tool and practical experience in its implementation are thought by some to be important factors contributing to less extreme swings in economic activity.[11]

### *Monetary Policy*

Why give fiscal policy all the credit (or even top billing)? Not only monetary theory but also the power of the monetary authority have advanced to the point where another episode like the Great Depression is absolutely avoidable.[12] Although the Federal Reserve System was established in 1913, it was, for many years, a weak institution, subservient to the Treasury Department and shackled by the Gold Standard. After World War II, the Fed gained the authority and the policy tools (not to mention the appropriate data) to "lean against the wind"—that is, to increase the growth rate of the money supply during slow-downs and to decrease its growth rate to prevent inflation during a recovery.

The efficacy of monetary policy, and also fiscal policy, in promoting economic stability is highly contentious. Perhaps the best that can be said here has already been articulated:

One of the most discussed [ideas] is that discretionary demand management (fiscal and monetary policy) has become more sophisticated and effective in reducing cyclical instability. This is obviously a critical issue but also one very difficult to test. Most observers would likely agree that some successes were scored by United States monetary and fiscal policies in the 1950s and 1960s but that the record was mixed and marked by increasing errors on the inflationary side. (Zarnowitz and Moore, in Gordon [1986], p. 536)

Both monetary and fiscal policy are far from perfect in managing economic activity. Indeed, many would describe them as clumsy or totally ineffective. Some would go so far as to say, because of the time lags involved and poor implementation, fiscal and monetary activism exacerbate business fluctuations. Controversial as they may be, demand-management policies can have profound effects on the economy.[13] And, in fact, not many professional forecasters would like to formulate their predictions without knowledge of the current policy environment.

### A Restructured Economy

Zarnowitz and Moore offer yet another explanation for the dampened amplitude of cyclical fluctuations since World War II.[14] These experts attribute such dampening to the changing structure of the U.S. economy. Since World War II, the U.S. economy has become more service-oriented. There is more employment and production in industries such as retail trade, finance, insurance, and real estate. Government jobs have also increased drastically in the postwar era. The jobs in these industries are less sensitive to cyclical fluctuations than are jobs in manufacturing and construction. The evolution toward the service sector, and away from manufacturing, has resulted in an economy that is not as cyclically sensitive as was the case before the war years.

### Other Explanations for Dampened Fluctuations

Automatic stabilizers, monetary and fiscal policy, and a restructured economy have all been suggested to explain the diminished amplitude of business fluctuations. These are the better-known explanations. Several less prominent, but worthy, hypotheses should be mentioned.

Galbraith's hypothesis is that a new sort of economic entity—the technostructural firm—has promoted macroeconomic stability in the postwar era.[15]

Several authors have used decreased wage and price flexibility after World War II to explain the dampened fluctuations.[16] This explanation may appear counterintuitive, since wage and price flexibility, at least in theory, has been associated with improved economic performance. But these authors argue that wage and price rigidity is a symptom of business cycles that are not so severe. The cycle is not as severe because the mechanisms that propagate the cycle, the dynamics of the economy, are more drawn out. The sluggish dynamics of the macroeconomy are reflected in less flexible wages and prices.

It is often prudent in situations such as these, where several explanations are offered for the same phenomenon, to take an eclectic view. It could very well be that all the hypotheses mentioned here have contributed to the observed decline in amplitude, perhaps some more than others. A strikingly different perspective, however, has been put forward by Christina Romer (1989). Romer's research suggests that the severity of economic fluctuations has not diminished in the postwar era. She reached this conclusion by working with, and revising, the prewar data on the U.S. economy.[17] We must remember that estimates of economic activity are just that—estimates. Simon Kuznets, who won the Nobel Prize in Economics for his efforts, developed estimates of economic activity for the United States going back to the 1860s. For the earlier years, the estimates were based on scanty and sometimes inconsistent data, which were all that was available. Working with the same raw data, Romer has developed alternate estimates for the prewar era that exhibit less severe fluctuations than Kuznets' series. Romer's prewar business cycles are just slightly more severe than those of the postwar period. These results, needless to say, put quite a damper on the view that the economy has become more stable in the modern era. But this is far from the final word on the issue. Other statistical research has already emerged that challenges Romer's results.[18] And more evidence on both sides is sure to be forthcoming.[19]

## Business-Cycle Theories

Having reviewed various hypotheses to explain the diminished amplitude of business cycles in the postwar U.S. economy (if, indeed, they have diminished), the reader should be impressed by the number of factors that can affect cyclical behavior. Income taxes, welfare programs, monetary and fiscal policy, the flexibility of wages and prices, the structure of the economy and the firms within it are all important factors. But these hypotheses have been used to explain the long-term changes in the business cycle. We now turn our attention to the factors or hypotheses that can explain why cycles exist in the first place. Why do modern economies not grow, or decline, at an even clip?

Something that surges forward and then retreats in an irregular fashion can be extremely difficult to predict. If the factors that cause business cycles—their roots—were known, then forecasting would be facilitated. It is not very delimiting to know that fluctuations occur in all economies, even those that are not market-oriented. If more were understood about the cause of business cycles, it might be possible to predict their dynamics.

Unfortunately, there are so many various theoretical explanations for economic fluctuations that any one theory is immediately suspect. Once again, any reasonable observer is bound to take the eclectic view—that there are a variety of causal factors, some more relevant than others depending on the circumstances. Thus, experts in business-cycle theory do not have a major advantage in economic forecasting. They do, however, have a substantial advantage over those who are ignorant of the factors that can give rise to nonperiodic fluctuations—they understand the dynamics of the business cycle. Moreover, to be a true eclectic, one must appreciate the individual theories that comprise the collection.

## Classification Schemes

There are enough contributors to, and theories concerning, business cycles that several modes of classification are possible. There are purely monetary theories (associated most closely with Hawtrey), monetary overinvestment theories (Hayek), nonmonetary overinvestment theories (Spiethoff), or, to use another classification system, pre-Keynesian, Keynesian, and post-Keynesian theories. Some theories may be classified as endogenous—business cycles arise from forces operating within the system; others exogenous—outside forces impact the system and give rise to fluctuations. These classification schemes are unimportant for the brief foray into business-cycle theory we shall make here (although it does sound impressive to say one is studying endogenous, post-Keynesian, overinvestment theories of the business cycle).

More important is the knowledge that economic fluctuations can, and probably do, result from a variety of sources. What are those sources and how do they generate cycles? Often, it will be expedient to alter the preceding question slightly to read, "What are the causes of economic slowdowns and how do these forces operate?" since the same forces working in the opposite manner would explain the onset of the expansion.

### Money and Credit

Certainly one of the most pervasive concepts used to explain contractions in economic activity is money and credit.[20] Toward the end of an expansion, credit is tight for a variety of reasons. Consumers and businesses may have borrowed heavily during the expansion when optimism and well-being were rife. The pool of loanable funds has, to a large extent, been drawn down. Moreover, financial institutions are wary of making further loans to creditors already saddled with debt. In such a situation, interest rates would rise, perhaps beyond some prohibitive threshold. Borrowing, and therefore spending, are reduced. Debts must be repaid. The diminished spending leads to unsold goods piling up in inventories and, eventually, to layoffs. The lost jobs, of course, imply further declines in income and the self-feeding process of economic decline begins.

There are a few criticisms concerning the analysis sketched above. One obvious query is: What has the Fed been doing through all this? The response: An increase in the money supply is not always effective in these circumstances. There may be a reluctance to increase the supply of money out of fear of inflation, which is typically evident at the later stages of an expansion. Moreover, it is not clear that more loans would occur if the Fed increased the pool of loanable funds. It would be like "pushing on a string" since the private sector, which is highly leveraged, is unwilling to take on further debt and banks are not willing to extend it. Finally, interest rates might actually rise as the Fed increases the pool of loanable funds under these circumstances. The money supply increase simply fuels inflationary expectations, causing lenders to raise nominal interest rates.[21] The increased rates for borrowing cause additional reductions in consumer and business spending.

Figure 2.4 **Percentage Change in the Money Supply** (M2)

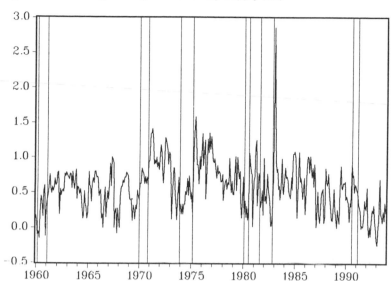

It is difficult to ignore the role of money with regard to economic slumps. Just about every recession is preceded by a decline in the growth rate of the money supply. With this information, one may wonder why it is so difficult to forecast eminent recessions. First, note that there are many declines in money growth with no ensuing slump. This, along with a time lag in data availability, diminishes the effectiveness of money growth as a signal of impending declines in economic activity. More will be said concerning money's value in predicting turning points in chapter 4. Here our concern is cause and effect, and simply because one event precedes another in time does not necessarily mean that the former causes the latter. Plenty of umbrellas are seen carried in the street before the rain, but all those umbrellas do not cause the rain. A third factor, the weather forecast, explains the presence of the umbrellas and the rain. By similar reasoning, there may be a third factor that explains the decreased money growth and the subsequent decline in economic activity.

Another fact that diminishes money's ability to explain recessions is that money growth is extremely erratic. Figure 2.4 indicates there are many precipitous declines in money growth that are not followed by recessions.

Thus, it is by no means certain that declines in money growth cause economic decline. And it is by no means certain that increases in the growth rate of the money supply can prevent a slow-down.

One final note on the supply of money: Nobel laureate Milton Friedman, among others, contends that a precipitous drop in the money supply was the primary cause of the Great Depression. This view is controversial for the reason just mentioned—a third factor, namely, a drop in the demand for loans and investment capital (due to bleak expectations), may have caused the declines in both money and economic activity. Yet almost everyone agrees that had the Fed been more adept in 1930,[22] the Depression would have been less severe.[23]

### *Expectations*

Pessimism on the part of consumers or businesses, a loss of confidence, can incite an economic slump. Negative perceptions about future income or profits can cause the private sector to pull in their horns, so to speak. The decline in spending leads to job losses and actual declines in income. Forecasting plays an important part here because it can foster expectations that become self-fulfilling. If households and firms believe, or are at least made uncertain by, dire forecasts of the immediate future, the flow of spending is reduced and the contractionary phase of the business cycle begins. If these ideas concerning the role of expectations are correct, then one should observe increased savings rates before recessions as income is socked away as a hedge against the uncertain future. It is not clear that this is the case. Savings rates typically increase during slumps, but it takes a generous eye to conclude that these rates increase beforehand[24] (see Figure 2.5).

Similarly, measures of consumer and business sentiment—surveys taken to access expectations—typically decline during the slump. Declines in consumer sentiment precede recessions well enough to be included in the Department of Commerce's index of leading indicators.

### *Keynes's Theory*

Keynes emphasized the importance of spending and its effects on overall economic activity. Yet, his formal explanation of the causes of business cycles involved the productivity of plant and equipment.[25] As an expansion progresses toward its peak, firms acquire more plant and equipment—capital—in order to increase production. Each new piece of capital, however, is not as productive as previous additions to the

Figure 2.5 **Personal Savings as a Percentage of Personal Income**

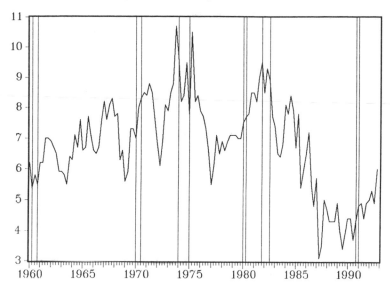

capital stock, perhaps because of crowding, or more likely, because of less maintenance and general human attention. Economists refer to this well-accepted concept as "diminishing marginal productivity." The concept does not imply that capital is not productive, just that the increase in productivity is not as great as for earlier capital acquisitions.

Another phenomenon likely to occur near the peak of an expansion is higher interest rates (as previously discussed). Consider, now, a firm deciding how much to spend on new plant and equipment. The productivity of the new capital is diminished, but the cost to finance its acquisition is high. Thus, near the peak of the cycle, firms are induced to cut their outlays for new plant and equipment. This leads to declines in employment and income in the capital-goods-producing industries, which mark the beginning of the contraction.

Keynes's theory of the business cycle can be classified as endogenous. All of the forces leading to the recurrent ups and downs in economic activity are part of the system. No outside force, such as a decline in confidence, or an unwarranted drop in the money supply, is needed to begin or to sustain the dynamics of the process. Business fluctuations occur, at least to the Keynesian way of thinking, because of forces that are inherent within the economy.

Samuelson and Hicks also have developed endogenous theories of the business cycle.[26] Both economists demonstrate how nonperiodic cycles will result in an economy where business and household spending feed off one another. The basic idea is that business spending depends, to a large extent, on increases in household spending. Now, when businesses spend to acquire plant and equipment this generates income, a given fraction of which is spent by consumers. From this terse description, it may appear that this system will result in ever-increasing levels of spending and income for businesses and households. This does not occur because the increments in consumer spending dwindle over time. This, in turn, causes a decline in business spending. The system results in nonperiodic fluctuations in overall economic activity.

### *Innovation*

The importance of the endogenous theories of the business cycle lies in their implication that fluctuations are an inherent characteristic of the economy. Outside forces are not required to generate cycles. It is most likely, however, that exogenous forces contribute to the cyclical behavior observed in the real world. We now examine some of these exogenous factors, beginning with technology and innovation.[27]

The idea that innovation spurs economic growth and results in business cycles can be traced back to Schumpeter, who had a rather broad definition of innovation, namely: "changes in methods of production and transportation, or changes in industrial organization, or in the production of a new article, or in the opening up of new markets or new sources of material."[28]

The innovations Schumpeter spoke of could spawn prosperity, but eventually they would lead to falling prices because of increased productivity. The falling prices are good for consumers, but, in the long run, profits are driven down, leading to the contraction. Today there is little controversy in asserting that technological advances that enhance productivity affect economic growth. These advances certainly come in fits and starts ("swarms," to use Schumpeter's word) and that coincides nicely with irregular cycles of growth.

More controversial is the notion that these advances contain the seeds of the next recession. Schumpeter emphasized the increased business spending that follows on the heels of innovation. Once that wave of spending subsides, slower growth in conjunction with falling profit margins heralds the downturn.

### Supply Shocks

Another exogenous force that has the potential to cause recessions is interruptions in the supply of resources. The most notable example of this is the 1973–75 recession. The consensus is that this lengthy contraction was caused by the sharp curtailment in the supply of oil purposely arranged by the OPEC oil cartel.

Natural disasters, strikes, and wars[29] are all examples of supply shocks. The effects of these shocks are doubly pernicious because they result in stagflation—a recession coupled with inflation. This was certainly the case in the 1973–75 recession. It is difficult to imagine another scenario where the supply of such a crucial resource would be cut so sharply.

Unfortunately, understanding that supply shocks can cause economic fluctuations is of little use to forecasters since these shocks are, by their very nature, unforeseen. When supply shocks do occur, the forecast is for stagflation in the immediate future.

### Politics

Another exogenous factor that may impinge upon the economic system and generate business cycles is politics. Various writers have suggested that an upcoming election is bound to bring forth stimulative economic policies with short-term results. The longer-term consequences of these policies are felt after the election.

It is not clear that the Fed has acted expansively a majority of the time prior to presidential elections. It is difficult, however, to dismiss such charges in some cases—the 1992 election is such a case.

We still face the question, raised earlier, of the efficacy and timing of monetary and fiscal policy. Are these policies that effective, and are politicians that adept at implementing them? Certainly not with fiscal policy. Perhaps with monetary policy, politicians have unwittingly set off business cycles in their zeal for reelection.

### Foreign Economies

Foreign economies can exert forces that result in fluctuations in the domestic economy. There is a body of literature concerning the transmission of these forces. The more prevalent foreign trade and investment are in the domestic economy, the more important these factors will be.

The volume of imports and exports, exchange rates, and the level of interest rates relative to those in other nations all play a role here.

The demand for our exports declines when the countries to which we export experience a recession. The diminished demand for these products can result in layoffs and declines in domestic income. Thus, the foreign recession is transmitted to the domestic economy.

### Sun Spots

It would be remiss if we did not mention one of the most ancient ideas, now largely disregarded, concerning the source of business fluctuations—agricultural harvests. A poor harvest is the harbinger of a slump as agricultural misfortune is passed on to the other sectors of the economy. Perhaps not. It could be that a lean harvest, which results in high prices for food, would stimulate work effort and touch off an economic boom. The theoreticians have never resolved the issue of whether a poor harvest culminates in a recession or an expansion. In any event, it causes a cyclical fluctuation.

The diminished relative size of the agricultural sector has undoubtedly pushed these ideas into the background.[30] However, there is a lesson to be learned here about taking things a step too far. It was the misfortune of W. Stanley Jevons (1835–82), a prominent economist in his day, to ascribe the fluctuations in crop yields to sun spots. Hence, the sunspot theory of the business cycle.

### Inventories

In economics, the term "investment" means business spending on plant and equipment plus the change in business inventories. It makes sense to include inventory changes with spending on new capital because, when a firm increases its inventory of raw materials or finished products, it has gained a valuable productive asset. Inventory changes play a crucial role in the writings of many business-cycle analysts. Indeed, some analysts refer to business cycles as inventory cycles.

In response to bloated inventories, firms may cut production and employment. This leads to further declines in income and a general contraction. Eventually, inventories become thin and the expansion begins, as firms, uncomfortable with the low level of finished-goods inventories, expand production.

Despite the critical role played by inventories in the above analysis, their part is passive in the sense that their behavior is more a symptom than a cause of the cycle. Why had inventories become bloated in the first place? A lack of demand brought on by higher interest rates or bleak expectations? In essence, inventories served as a buffer—absorbing production that was not sold. Yet, inventories are not a very effective buffer in the U.S. economy given that overall sales fluctuate more widely than production. Moreover, if climbing inventories cause recessions, then one must explain why the inventory-to-sales ratio typically continues to climb until well after the recession has begun.

### Price Changes and Equilibrium Business-Cycle Theory

Prices certainly play a part in business-cycle analysis, usually as some sort of propagation mechanism. Theoretically, the price level is procyclical in nature—increasing more rapidly during expansions and less rapidly, or even falling, during contractions (except in the case of stagflation). We have already noted how prices and wages were seen to fluctuate more severely during the prewar era in the United States. This, it was suggested, might be responsible for the diminished severity of business cycles in the postwar period.

The most recent contribution to the explanation of business cycles originates with Robert Lucas (1981) and casts price changes in a pivotal role. Lucas's theory is based on the controversial ideas of "rational expectations" and "market clearing." Nevertheless, the essential elements of this compelling explanation are, in the author's own words, "embarrassingly simple."

To begin, a given producer in the economy will not regard all price changes, even if they are of the same magnitude, in the same light. There are price changes, and then there are *price changes*. To be more forthcoming, a producer will react differently to price changes that are expected to be permanent.

Imagine a price increase that producers expect to be temporary. With an eye toward making larger profits, production is stepped up. But the increase in production is accomplished by using existing plant and equipment more intensely. There is no point in acquiring more capital. By the time the new plant and equipment come on line, the high price will have vanished (or, at least, it is expected to be so).

Also, firms are not likely to acquire additions to their capital stock in the face of price increases for their products if other prices are rising just as rapidly. There are no real gains to be made by expanding production when the prices of capital, labor, and other commodities are also increasing.

Hence, firms desire to increase their productive capacity through capital expansion when the price of their product increases permanently and relative to other commodities. But there is the rub, for it is difficult to discern whether a given price increase is permanent and relative.

Industry consultants and price forecasters can, and are, hired to help with this problem. But that does not preclude the possibility of incorrect decisions. Even when it is inappropriate, the decision to expand expenditures on plant and equipment stimulates economic activity. But unwarranted expansions contain the seeds of the next contraction: when the price increase is finally perceived to be merely on a par with other price and cost increases, or disappears altogether, the retrenchment begins.

Nothing that has been said here is a radical departure from many of the well-established theories concerning recurrent fluctuations. But the foundations of Lucas's theory (equilibrium business-cycle theory), which have not been spelled out here, lie in the neoclassical assumptions of market clearing and rational expectations. The controversy surrounding the foundations has prevented the theory's wide acceptance.[31]

Finally, one may ask what gives rise to the price changes in the first place. The response of rational expectations theorists is exogenous shocks. Thus, equilibrium business-cycle theory is classified as an exogenous theory of economic fluctuations.

**Summary**

For our purposes, how a particular business-cycle theory is classified makes little difference. Yet, in summarizing the various theories, it is convenient to designate them as either endogenous or exogenous. Exogenous business-cycle theories can have endogenous elements (see Table 2.2).

Typically, the exogenous factor—let us take innovation as an example—affects business spending, which then transmits the shock to the rest of the economy. Indeed, the volatility of business spending and its

Table 2.2

**Causal Factors in Economic Fluctuations**

| Endogenous | Exogenous |
|---|---|
| Money and credit | Expectations |
| Marginal productivity of capital—Keynes | Innovation |
| | Supply shocks |
| Interaction of household and business spending—Samuelson | Politics |
| | Foreign economies |
| | Agricultural yields |
| | Price changes—Equilibrium business-cycle theory |

potential impact on overall economic activity make it a prime candidate for the conveyor of exogenous shocks.

In the lingo of business-cycle theorists, exogenous theories of the business cycle have an "impulse" mechanism and a "propagation" mechanism. The former is what we have been calling the exogenous shock and the latter is the apparatus that transmits the shock.

It should be apparent by now that business cycles differ with respect to their depth, duration, and dispersion. The explanations for these unique disturbances are manifold, with no single theory predominating.

Some of these theories rely on outside forces, which are typically magnified by the economic system, to generate cycles. Since the exogenous shocks are random and vary in magnitude, the cyclical patterns are also random and vary in magnitude.

Other explanations demonstrate the possibility that irregular cycles can emanate solely from the internal churning of the economic system.[32]

The multifarious causes and nonuniformity of the business cycle make economic forecasting a hazardous endeavor. The turning points are especially difficult to foresee. Once a turning point has been established, the task of projection is scarcely made any easier. Economic aggregates—production, income, prices, unemployment, profits, sales, interest rates, and the like—are not liable to behave as they did in the previous expansion or contraction.

Nevertheless, acquaintance with the typical behavior of these aggregates over the course of the cycle is useful, just as it is best to be familiar with business-cycle theory. Economic cycles may eschew uniformity and defy explanation, but any information about their behavior or their origins might be of use in forecasting.

## Notes

1. See Staller (1958) concerning business cycles in socialist economies.

2. An old joke defines a "recession" as when your neighbor is unemployed, a "crisis" as when you are unemployed, and a "depression" as when your spouse is out of work.

3. As a measure of economic performance, GDP does have drawbacks. For instance, it reflects no attempt to adjust for environmental damage or changes in the quality of life.

4. The statistical evidence disputes these assertions. Studies have shown no relationships between the depth, duration, and dispersion of one phase of the business cycle and the subsequent phase. See McNees (1992).

5. Burns and Mitchell (1946) is the classic study of the typical behavior of macroeconomic variables over the business cycle. See Evans (1969) for a more recent analysis.

6. Falling prices have been associated with contractions, but the last time prices fell in a meaningful way was during the 1948–49 recession. Some, but not all, of the subsequent contractions have coincided with *disinflation*—a reduction in the rate of inflation—as opposed to *deflation*—falling prices.

7. The 1973–75 recession is a notable exception.

8. See Evans (1969) for a good example.

9. Burns (1960) is the classic source for this observation.

10. Moore (1983, ch. 8) presents evidence that automatic stabilizers work better mitigating downturns than limiting exuberant expansions.

11. See Friedman and Heller (1969). On p. 30, Heller cites evidence supporting the role of fiscal policy in reducing the amplitude of business cycles.

12. Again, see Friedman and Heller (1969, p. 79). This book is a transcription of a debate between the two. Friedman, of course, supports the view that changes in the money supply have a more profound effect on the macroeconomy than does fiscal policy (which is championed by Heller).

13. A recent study promotes monetary policy as a way of fighting contractions and also credits, to a lesser extent, fiscal policy and automatic stabilizers. See Romer and Romer (1994).

14. Zarnowitz and Moore's article appears in Gordon (1986). See pp. 536–39.

15. See Ramsey (1980, p. 24) for a summary and critique of Galbraith's argument.

16. See Taylor's article and that of Delong and Summers, both in Gordon (1986).

17. Sheffrin (1988) finds that business-cycle severity has not diminished in the postwar period for five out of six European countries that he considered in his study.

18. See Balke and Gordon (1989).

19. Diebold and Rudebusch (1992) note that contractions have become shorter and expansions longer in the postwar period. They consider whether this in itself has resulted in milder fluctuations.

20. See Friedman's paper in Gordon (1986) for more details than those presented here concerning money and credit as a source of economic fluctuations.

21. This is known as the Fisher effect, after Irving Fisher.

22. The Federal Reserve did not have as strict a control on the money supply as it has today, nor adequate data concerning money in the 1930s.

23. See Temin (1989) for insight into the causes of the Great Depression.

24. Gross private savings as a percentage of GDP declined markedly just before the recession that began in July 1990.

25. "It is by reason of the existence of durable equipment that the economic future is linked to the present" (Keynes, 1973, p. 146).

26. See Samuelson (1939) or Sorkin (1988, pp. 45–50).

27. Some writers consider technological innovation an endogenous factor. The economic environment dictates the rate of technological advance. Kondratieff was such a writer. See Van Duijn (1983, p. 66).

28. The quote is from Schumpeter (1927, p. 295). Schumpeter's classic work on business cycles, however, is the two-volume set (Schumpeter 1939).

29. This provides an opportunity to lay to rest the notion that war is good for the economy. Wars are supply shocks that result in stagflation; hence, the need for price controls during wars. The war itself is detrimental to economic activity. What can stimulate the economy is the increased spending on national defense. This amounts to a massive fiscal stimulus. The result would be even more expansive if the same amount of spending on national defense had been undertaken during peace time.

30. Poor crop yields in 1973 may have contributed to the 1973–75 recession. See Sorkin (1988, p. 65).

31. Despite the shallowness of this explanation of equilibrium business-cycle theory, one can find debilities. Why would all producers mistakenly view a temporary price increase as permanent and inappropriately expand the capital stock? It stands to reason that the mistaken perceptions of some producers would be matched by mistakes in the other direction by other producers. Because of the assumptions made by rational expectations theorists, this sort of canceling of the errors is not possible. See Plosser (1989) for an accessible review of equilibrium business-cycle theory.

32. See Bratt (1937) for a quirky exposition of the causes of business cycles.

## References

Balke, Nathan S., and Gordon, Robert J. 1989. "The Estimation of Prewar Gross National Product: Methodology and New Evidence." *Journal of Political Economy* (February): 38–92.

Bratt, Elmer C. 1937. *Business Cycles and Forecasting.* Chicago: Business Publications.

Burns, Arthur F. 1960. "Progress toward Economic Stability." *American Economic Review* (March): 1–19.

Burns, Arthur F., and Mitchell, Wesley C. 1946. *Measuring Business Cycles.* New York: NBER.

Diebold, Francis X., and Rudebusch, Glenn D. 1992. "Have Postwar Economic Fluctuations Been Stabilized?" *American Economic Review* (September): 993–1018.

Evans, Michael K. 1969. *Macroeconomic Activity: Theory, Forecasting, and Control*. New York: Harper and Row.

Friedman, Milton, and Heller, Walter W. 1969. *Monetary vs. Fiscal Policy*. New York: W.W. Norton.

Gordon, Robert J., ed. 1986. *The American Business Cycle*. Chicago: University of Chicago Press.

Keynes, John M. 1973. *The General Theory of Employment, Interest, and Money. The Collected Writings of John Maynard Keynes,* vol. 7. London: Macmillan.

Lucas, Robert E. 1981. *Studies in Business Cycle Theory*. Cambridge, MA: MIT Press.

McNees, Stephen K. 1992. "The 90–91 Recession in Historical Perspective." *New England Economic Review* (January–February): 3–22.

Moore, Geoffrey H. 1983. *Business Cycles, Inflation, and Forecasting*. Cambridge, MA: Ballinger.

Plosser, Charles I. 1989. "Understanding Real Business Cycles." *Journal of Economic Perspectives* (Summer): 51–77.

Romer, Christina D. 1989. "The Prewar Business Cycle Reconsidered: New Estimates of Gross National Product, 1869–1908." *Journal of Political Economy* (February): 1–37.

Romer, Christina D., and Romer, David H. 1994. "What Ends Recessions?" In S. Fischer and J. Rottemberg (eds.), *NBER Macroeconomics Annual,* vol. 9, pp. 13–57. Cambridge, MA: MIT Press.

Samuelson, Paul. 1939. "Interactions between the Multiplier Analysis and the Principle of Acceleration." *Review of Economics and Statistics* 21: 75–78.

Schumpeter, Joseph. 1927. "The Explanation of the Business Cycle." *Economica* (December): 286–311.

———. 1939. *Business Cycles,* vols. 1 and 2. New York: McGraw-Hill.

Sheffrin, Steven M. 1988. "Have Economic Fluctuations Been Dampened? A Look at Evidence outside the United States." *Journal of Monetary Economics* (January): 73–83.

Sorkin, Alan L. 1988. *Monetary and Fiscal Policy and Business Cycles in the Modern Era*. Lexington, MA: D.C. Heath.

Staller, George. 1958. "Fluctuations in Planned and Free-Market Economies." *American Economic Review* (June): 385–95.

Temin, Peter. 1989. *Lessons from the Great Depression*. Cambridge, MA: MIT Press.

Van Duijn, Jacob J. 1983. *The Long Wave in Economic Life*. London: George Allen and Unwin.

*3*

# Long Waves

> I have seen in my long life a lot of people burn their fingers over discoveries of cycles. The discoverer "sees things" almost as bizarre as drunkards. Once we were satisfied that "the" cycle was ten years in length and since that was smashed, we have had almost every other conceivable discovery.
>
> —Irving Fisher, 1946

As it stands today, and throughout most of its development, wave theory has been held in ill repute by the economics profession. Yet, the idea that economic activity exhibits long-lived waves that are somewhat uniform in their duration has fascinated many and attracted the attention of most forecasters. These waves of economic activity are not easily discerned. Typically, the data must be massaged and then viewed with a generous eye to perceive the undulations.

Regardless of their obscurity, if these waves exist, any forecaster would want to know of them. We shall see, however, that the application of wave theory to the practical matter of making specific forecasts is rather limited. Nevertheless, these applications often result in dramatic prognostications that have broad implications for the economy. Moreover, an investigation of long waves will shed further light on the nature and causes of the business cycle.

## Introduction

In 1930, Nikolai Dmitriyevitch Kondratieff was exiled to Siberia allegedly because of his involvement with an unsanctioned political party.

Table 3.1

**Average Annual Growth Rate of Industrial Production in the United States for Selected Periods**

| Years | Phase | Duration (years) | Growth rate (percent) |
|-------|-------|------------------|------------------------|
| 1860–90 | Upswing | 31 | 5.3 |
| 1890–1929 | Downswing | 30 | 4.4 |
| 1929–48 | Upswing | 20 | 7.3 |
| 1948–75 | Downswing | 28 | 4.4 |

*Sources:* U.S. Department of Commerce, and author's calculations.

The true cause of Kondratieff's exile was his investigation into long waves of economic activity. His findings contradicted Marxist political doctrine. He was never heard from again.

Working mainly with time series on prices, bolstered with some financial data, Kondratieff was able to discern cycles of economic activity lasting fifty to sixty years in England, France, and the United States. The contradiction with Marxist dogma is obvious: If capitalist economies are expected to oscillate between good periods and bad over the long haul of history, what does that imply about Marx's prognosis of capitalism's iminent collapse?

Seventy years later, the idea that economic activity ebbs and flows in long waves is better tolerated, but far from wide acceptance. If long-lived waves exist, they lurk in the background, exuding their subtle effects on the business cycle.

Table 3.1 is an attempt to identify long waves in economic growth. From 1860 until 1890, industrial production in the United States grew at an average annual rate of 5.3 percent. From 1890 until 1929, growth averaged only 4.4 percent per year before shooting up to 7.3 percent in the period from 1929 to 1948. Are these the ebb and flow of Kondratieff's waves?

Wave theorists also consider cycles of shorter duration than Kondratieff's. The most well established of the shorter cycles are the Kitchin or inventory cycle, the Juglar cycle, and Kuznets's cycle. As we shall see, each type of cycle is associated with a different form of business spending. When wave theorists argue among themselves, the argument typically concerns whether all these cycles are interrelated or independent, and the dates of their peaks and troughs.

Figure 3.1 **The Kitchin Cycle—Change in Business Inventories**

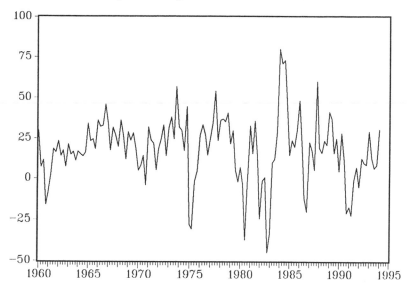

## The Kitchin Cycle

The Kitchin cycle is associated with inventories.[1] From trough to peak, inventories accumulate as production advances. Perhaps because of over-optimism, inventory growth outstrips final demand and, in response, production is cut. Inventories dwindle from the peak to the trough of the Kitchin cycle. The whole cycle, from trough to trough, is surmised to last forty to sixty months.

For the U.S. economy, the troughs in inventory investment conform, to a certain extent, to this hypothesized behavior and timing. It is not clear that the dip in inventories in late 1970 was a genuine trough. Even if it was, it came 120 months after the previous trough. It would appear that the Kitchin cycle missed a beat. The trough that occurs in late 1982 is only twenty-seven months after the 1980 trough—an extra beat (see Figure 3.1).

Since the change in business inventories is somewhat erratic, one could take a moving average of the data. This would smooth out any minor movements and perhaps make the true peaks and troughs more apparent. Doing so in this case would not substantially alter the analysis. Notice that troughs in the change in inventories roughly coincide

Figure 3.2 **The Kitchin Cycle—Change in Business Inventories** (six-quarter moving average)

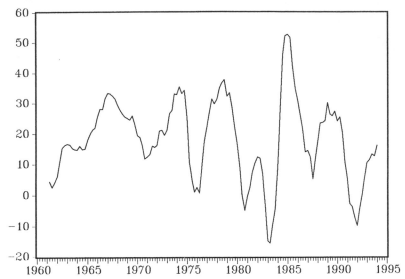

with business-cycle troughs as determined by the NBER Business Cycle Dating Committee. The only exception to this is the inventory trough that occurred late in 1986. Even in this instance, economic activity slowed markedly before resuming normal rates of growth in early 1987, although an official recession was never declared (see Figure 3.2).

We may consider other forms of inventory data. A more uniform Kitchin cycle may emerge if we consider, say, the ratio of inventories to final sales. Such data certainly do provide a different assessment of inventory behavior (Figure 3.3).

The troughs in this series, which has been smoothed with a six-quarter moving average, are roughly five years apart, with an extra dip that appears only two years after the 1980 trough. The peaks in the ratio of inventories to final sales, however, coincide to a certain extent with business-cycle peaks. The Department of Commerce classifies the inventory to sales ratio as a lagging indicator and its peaks do indeed seem to occur just after business-cycle peaks as defined by the NBER.

Given this evidence, inventory behavior and economic activity appear to be related. The determination of which variable is the cause and which is the effect requires a more sophisticated analysis. The reader is

Figure 3.3 **The Kitchin Cycle—Inventory-to-Sales Ratio** (six-quarter moving average)

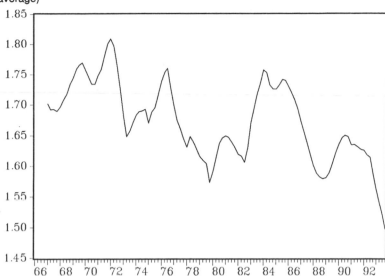

left to judge whether the periodicity of the inventory cycles presented here is enough to assert the existence of a Kitchin cycle.

Considering the change in inventory data presented in Figures 3.1 and 3.2, since a trough was last reached in late 1991, we might expect another to occur in late 1996 or early 1997. Since these troughs correspond with troughs in business cycles, an economic contraction would be slated to begin about then. If this scenario does not pan out, wave theorists could assert that the Kitchin cycle was dominated by another type of long wave, such as the Juglar cycle.

**The Juglar Cycle**

The Juglar cycle is expected to last seven to eleven years from trough to trough.[2] It is related to business spending on durable equipment, which is expected to occur in clumps because of the natural deterioration of such equipment and the possibility of speeding up or putting off actual purchases in accordance with product demand and finance charges. Technological innovation may also cause bunching in expenditures by firms on durable capital.

Brisk consumer demand, low interest rates, or new technologies cause a spate of spending on durable equipment by producers as the

Figure 3.4 **The Juglar Cycle—Spending on Producers' Durables**

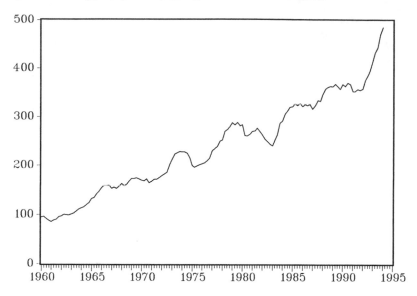

Juglar cycle begins. This sort of spending fuels gains in income and profits, and the prosperity of the capital-goods industry is passed on to the rest of the economy. Eventually, businesses overreact by purchasing more equipment than is warranted, or consumer demand or interest rates become unfavorable, and the downward phase of the Juglar begins. At this point, firms are well stocked with productive capital. It could be many years until the trough is reached.

In order to discern the Juglar cycle, it is insufficient simply to regard producers' expenditures on durable equipment. Even if these figures are adjusted for inflation, they have a significant upward trend owing to growth in the size of the economy (see Figure 3.4).

A trend line is fitted to the raw data and the deviations from the trend are taken. After this, a moving average may be taken to smooth over the irregularities[3] (see Figures 3.5 and 3.6).

The troughs in these massaged data on producers' durable spending appear to conform to the timing suggested by Juglar. There are almost ten years between the trough in the early 1960s and the subsequent one in the early 1970s. The remaining troughs vary from five to eight years apart. These troughs occur two or three years after business-cycle troughs as declared by the NBER. The peaks roughly coincide with the

Figure 3.5 **The Juglar Cycle—Spending on Producers' Durables** (deviations from trend)

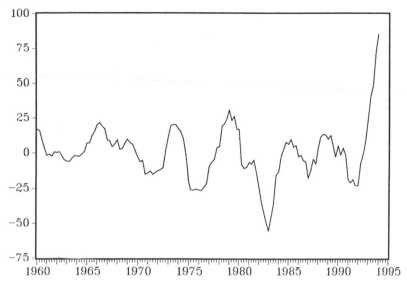

Figure 3.6 **The Juglar Cycle—Spending on Producers' Durables** (six-quarter moving average of deviations from trend)

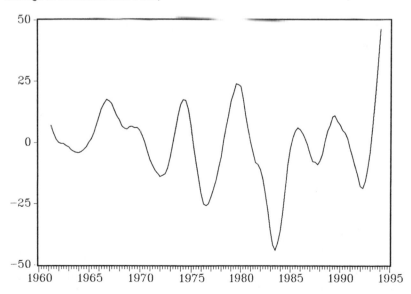

onset of economic contractions. (The peak in the mid-1960s warrants the use of the word "roughly.") Given this rhythm, one would expect, and indeed finds, a Juglar trough around 1993, two years after the business-cycle trough of March 1991. Since Juglar peaks coincide with recessions and may be expected to occur four to five years after the Juglar trough, the next recession is slated for 1998 or so.

This is in contrast to the date suggested by the Kitchin cycle—late 1996. Wave theorists recognize these sorts of contradictions and usually resolve them by suggesting that the longer wave—in this case the Juglar—will dominate. Moreover, the dates suggested by wave theories are merely rough-and-ready estimates since their periodicity is not exact.

The irregularities in the duration of the waves thwarts their usefulness in forecasting. However, if two or more waves indicate the same date for a slump in economic activity, it is referred to as a "conjuncture." The Great Depression is often pointed to as a conjuncture of Kitchin, Juglar, Kuznets, and Kondratieff waves.

**The Kuznets Cycle**

Kuznets cycles conform to investment in structures and are theorized to last twenty years or so.[4] The structures are both residential and nonresidential. Thus, Kuznets cycles refer to new homes, apartment and office buildings, factories, warehouses, and the like. The clustering of such expenditures can be explained on the same basis as that of producers' durable equipment: the actual expenditures can be postponed or advanced to conform with favorable demand or finance circumstances. Since structures last longer than durable equipment, the Kuznets cycle is expected to be longer than the Juglar (see Figure 3.7). The data on expenditures on structures must be detrended in order to uncover the cycles (Figure 3.8). A moving average also might be taken, but it is not clear that this makes the cycles more apparent in this instance (Figure 3.9).

Regardless of which chart we consider, the troughs appear to be much closer than the hypothesized twenty years. These troughs might be said to coincide, albeit very coarsely, with troughs in overall economic activity. The postwar U.S. data do not support the existence of Kuznets cycles to the same degree that they support Kitchin and Juglar cycles.[5]

Figure 3.7 **The Kuznets Cycle—Spending on Structures**

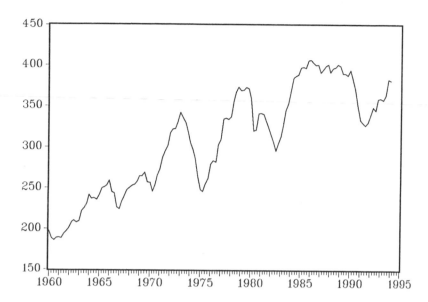

Figure 3.8 **The Kuznets Cycle—Spending on Structures** (deviations from trend)

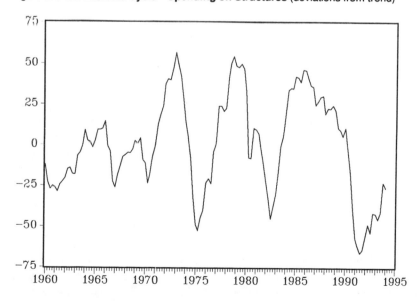

Figure 3.9 **The Kuznets Cycle—Spending on Structures** (six-quarter moving average of deviations from trend)

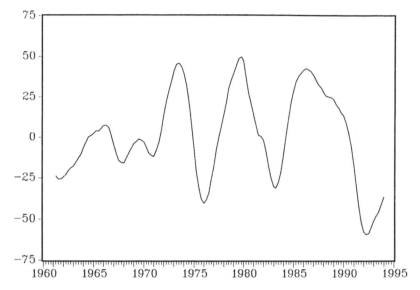

## Kondratieff Cycles

Kondratieff cycles, which are suspected to last anywhere from forty to seventy years, are perhaps the culmination of all three shorter cycles. Perhaps not. As mentioned, the interrelationships of the cycles are a matter of debate. Kondratieff himself mentions the shorter cycles only in passing. Schumpeter is credited with suggesting a scheme relating the cycles: one Kondratieff consists of six Juglars consisting of three Kitchins each.[6] Verification of this three-cycle scheme has been sketchy, just as verification of the individual cycles has not been totally convincing.

How well established are Kondratieff's long waves? Before we look at the evidence, we should reiterate that Kondratieff analyzed mostly data on prices.[7] With these figures, he was able to discern the long waves in some, but not all, of his variables. He associated the price waves with undulations in general economic activity. High prices implied high levels of economic activity, while low prices indicated slumps. This association has been disputed. Consider supply shocks such as a war or an oil embargo. These events tend simultaneously to raise prices and mitigate against economic growth. Rostow's investiga-

Figure 3.10 **Detrended Index of Business Activity in the United States**

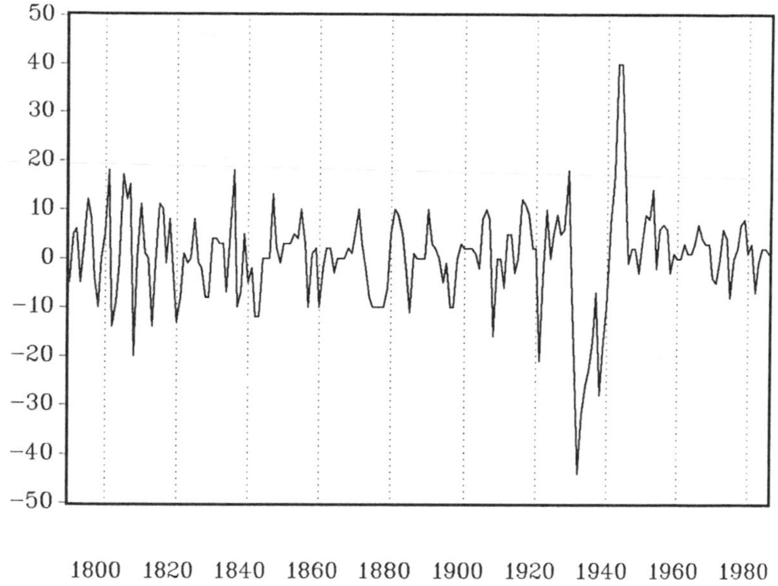

tion into long waves contradicts Kondratieff's association between high prices and high rates of economic growth.[8]

Nevertheless, the contentious association is not a major issue today since contemporary researchers have data, however imperfect, that reflect overall economic activity. The Federal Reserve Board's monthly index of industrial production begins in 1919. Before this date, researchers rely on the sketchy figures measuring production in various industries along with price data. From these numbers, broader measures of economic activity, usually production indexes, can be developed.[9] One such data set, computed by the AmeriTrust Corporation, represents detrended general business activity in the United States beginning in 1790[10] (see Figure 3.10).

Several comments are in order concerning Figure 3.10. First, it is apparent that no other contraction approaches the Great Depression in terms of severity. The most extreme expansion, on the other hand, occurred during World War II. If we ignore these two extremes, it is not obvious that business cycles have become less severe since World War II, a point that was discussed in chapter 2. The method by which the data were detrended can affect the variance of the resulting chart.

Table 3.2

**Growth Rates of Industrial Production in the United States**

| Phase | Dates | Growth rate (percent) |
|---|---|---|
| Upswing | 1864–73 | 6.2 |
| Downswing | 1873–95 | 4.7 |
| Upswing | 1895–1913 | 5.3 |
| Interruption [World War I] | | |
| Downswing | 1929–48 | 3.1 |
| Upswing | 1948–73 | 4.7 |

*Source*: Van Duijn (1983, p. 156).

But it is important to consider detrended figures, a point that was not lost on Kondratieff.[11] Finally, visual inspection of the detrended data does not reveal Kondratieff's waves (if they do, indeed, exist), as it did with some of the shorter cycles.

Kondratieff's waves may be uncovered by first identifying Juglar cycles and then combining five or six of these to form a Kondratieff. The average growth rates during the upswing and the downswing of the long wave may then be calculated.

One full Kondratieff wave would be an upswing and a downswing combined. Thus the first Kondratieff wave in the United States, according to Van Duijn, lasted thirty-two years, from 1864 to 1895. This is shorter than the hypothesized duration of forty to sixty years. Given the most recent upswing delineated in Table 3.2, the United States currently may be experiencing a downswing. Or perhaps this downswing ended with the recession in the early 1990s. It is too early to tell. Also notice that the timing suggested by Van Duijn in Table 3.2 is quite different from that suggested in Table 3.1. Yet both tables yield plausible growth rates for upswings and downswings. The fact that different scholars suggest different dates for Kondratieff's cycles does not help in delineating them. It really does pay, however, to have the most recent upswing end in 1973 and most wave analysts concur on this date.

Wave theorists have some reservations about the attempt made here to discern Kondratieff cycles in the United States. First, they applaud the fact that the data are based on industrial production. This is where, wave theorists contend, the long waves will be most apparent. But the figures should be per capita to erase the effects of population growth. It

Table 3.3

**Growth Rates of World Industrial Production**

| Phase | Dates | Growth rate (percent) |
|---|---|---|
| Upswing | 1845–72 | 4.6 |
| Downswing | 1872–92 | 3.0 |
| Upswing | 1892–1929 | 3.4 |
| Downswing | 1929–48 | 1.7 |
| Upswing | 1948–73 | 5.7 |

*Source*: Adapted from Van Duijn (1983, p. 154).

could be argued, however, that the detrending of the data handles that problem.

A more important concern of wave advocates is that the data are for only one country. Any given nation will have its own peculiar history, laws, and institutions. Long waves will be more easily observed if world industrial production is considered. At least economic growth in several major industrial countries can be combined to provide a more global perspective (see Table 3.3).

The first upswing in global economic activity begins in 1845 and lasts until 1872. The down phase is from 1872 until 1892, making a complete cycle lasting forty-eight years. The up phase from 1892 to 1929 includes World War I, while the subsequent downswing includes World War II. Kondratieff theorized that wars were most likely to occur on the upswing.[12] Despite the disruptions of the wars, the duration of this second wave is fifty-seven years, well within the prescribed bounds. The last upswing lasts twenty-six years ending in 1973. This implies a down phase lasting until the 1990s, perhaps longer.

Initially, Kondratieff offered no explanation for the long waves he discovered with the English, French, and American price data. This shortcoming was duly noted and remedied in Kondratieff's later papers.[13] His explanation involved the behavior of prices and interest rates over the long cycle. More specifically, the behavior of prices and interest rates encourages the clustering of business spending on plant and equipment resulting in the observed waves. Contemporary wave theorists place more emphasis on innovation (as defined by Schumpeter) and the resulting fluctuations in capital formation, especially infrastructure. In any event, business spending is called upon yet again by the wave theorists, this time to explain the longest wave.

## A Critique of Wave Theory

Any reasonable observer of the development of wave theory comes away with the impression that these analysts were strong on observation and identification, but rather weak in their theoretical explanations. Schumpeter, who developed the role of innovation in economic growth, is the exception. But Schumpeter's ideas are difficult to test. Long lists of innovations have been drawn up to determine if, and how, they are correlated with economic growth.[14] It is a fruitless exercise. Some innovations have larger impacts than others. The timing of these impacts does not necessarily correspond to the date attributed to each innovation. Moreover, the term "innovation" is used so broadly that experts would endlessly debate what institutional changes, technological advances, and product and market developments should be included on the list. And, in fact, researchers in this arena argue whether the innovations are bunched in the upswing of the wave or the downswing.

Wave theorists are nothing if not students of history. In the absence of a unifying theory of economic waves, historical events are used, in an ad hoc manner, as an explanatory device. Thus, World War I interrupted the up phase of a Kondratieff cycle, but World War II did not cause an interruption. That war fitted in nicely with the downswing. Exogenous shocks, such as wars or natural disasters, can be used as an excuse for not discerning uniform waves, or the waves occur in spite of those shocks. As another example, the oil shocks of the early 1970s are often highlighted as a major causal factor in the recession beginning in 1973. But to a wave theorist "it was not the oil crisis that brought an end to the great postwar expansion." Instead, "[a] gradual saturation of many manufacturing sector growth markets, coupled with a lack of major innovations" began the downswing of the Kondratieff cycle.[15] Hence, the 1973–75 recession was especially severe, according to wave theorists, because it coincided with the onset of the downswing of a Kondratieff wave.

The lack of a unified theory of long waves diminishes wave theory's usefulness in forecasting the economic future. For instance, if it is assumed that we are near the trough of the downswing that began in 1973, would a major war at this point postpone the upturn or would the upturn commence in any event? In a similar way, the fact that an individual nation, because of its particular circumstances, may experience a turning point before or after the general turning point hampers forecasting. Typically, forecasts are needed for individual nations, not so much for the world economy. The most important question concerns the length of the cycle in a given nation. Wave theorists, by their own admission, are not confident in their approach with regard to this question.

It does not help matters that these long waves are actually quite variable in length. Measured from trough to trough, one Kondratieff cycle has been observed to last forty-eight years while another lasted fifty-seven years. This is not precise enough for today's forecasting requirements. Will interest rates rise or fall next year? What will the unemployment rate be? Wave analysis has very little to offer in response to these sorts of questions.

Nevertheless, the investigation into long waves has provided some rewards. One of these rewards is a better understanding of the consequences of innovation and capital formation on economic growth. Another would be the suspicion that long waves are operating throughout the course of economic history. This knowledge may not be helpful for precise forecasts, but, if accepted, wave theory could influence forecasting. Recessions could be expected to be longer and more severe on the downswing. Expect major fluctuations near the turning points of the long wave.

Further research into wave theory is warranted. Advances, especially toward an explanation of the causes of long waves, would help our understanding of economic growth and could increase the accuracy of economic forecasts. The efforts of the System Dynamics Group at MIT are an example of such progress. They have shown that cycles of Kondratieff proportions can result from the dynamics of the production process.

## Batra's Wave Theory

We conclude this chapter with a review of Ravi Batra's book *The Great Depression of 1990*. Professor Batra uses wave theory to reach his conclusion that the U.S. economy will experience a major depression in the 1990s. Batra dismisses Kitchin, Juglar, Kuznets, and Kondratieff waves, calling them "irregular":

> The cycles we shall examine, however, are of a different type. They may be called regular or rhythmical cycles, because their patterns occur at regular intervals. (Batra, 1987, p. 21)

Figure 3.11 **Money Growth and Inflation Rates** (decade averages)

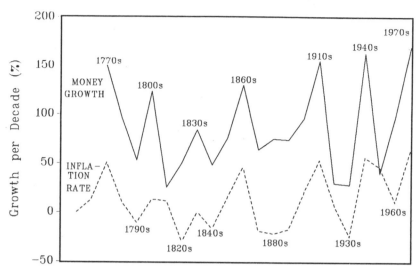

Indeed, Batra rather convincingly uncovers ten-year patterns in the rate of growth of the money supply, inflation, and government regulation. To discern the patterns, the raw data are averaged together by decade. Each decade has eleven years since the first year would be, for example, 1930 and the last 1940. The next decade would again include 1940 and run through 1950. The graph of decade-averaged money growth and inflation is shown in Figure 3.11.

A peak is achieved every third decade. With the 1970s as the most recent peak, money growth, inflation, and regulation are expected to peak again in the 2000s. Meanwhile, the three data series are expected to decline in the 1980s and a portion of the 1990s. These declines are the harbingers of the next Great Depression.

Obviously, this is a wave theory applied to make a rather dramatic forecast. This particular wave theory shares some characteristics with the others we have reviewed. For one thing, the explanation offered for Batra's waves is deficient. It is based on the "Law of Social Cycles" developed by Sarkar, an Indian mystic. Another shared characteristic is the use of exogenous shocks to explain aberrations in the waves. The 1890s should have been a peak decade, but were not. The disruptions resulting from the Civil War are invoked to explain the interruption of the pattern. The two world wars, however, did not have deleterious effects on the waves. Batra has more to offer, but before moving on, we should note that the 1970s were not a peak for money growth or inflation, as his chart anticipated that decade would be. At the time of publication of his book (1987), there were insufficient data to obtain the decade average for the 1980s. His pattern would be broken if the 1980s had a higher money growth and inflation rate than the 1970s. With these data now in hand, it is apparent that the 1970s were not a peak.

Curiously, Batra drops the decade-averaging technique when investigating the most important data series: detrended business activity in the United States. Instead, he considers the exact same chart we did earlier when attempting to discern Kondratieff's waves (Figure 3.9). The reader may reconsider that chart to verify the rule Batra develops:

> In the U.S. economy there has been at least one recession every decade, and a great depression every third or sixth decade in the sense that if the third decade managed to avoid a depression, then the sixth decade experienced a cumulative effect—an all-out disaster. (Batra, 1987, p. 107)

Now to apply the rule: The 1960s had one minor recession but avoided a depression. Thus, the 1990s will experience a cumulative effect—an all-out disaster. Notice that this analysis can be made to jibe with a Kondratieff cycle, which could be expected to attain a trough in the 1990s.

Since we have the same data as Batra, we may apply his decade-averaging technique to see if it confirms his rule and results in the same dire forecast for the 1990s.

Figure 3.12 makes it clear that the 1930s were an all-out disaster. There has never been a more dismal decade for business activity before or since. And the 1960s were, indeed, depression-free. In fact, the growth in business activity averaged out to be slightly above trend for the 1960s. According to Batra's rule, the 1990s should contain an all-out disaster. Thus, the decade-averaging technique verifies Batra's rule.

Again, one wonders why it was not applied to these data in his book. There are some minor discrepancies with Figure 3.12, and Figure 3.11, one which employed decade averages for money growth and inflation. The 1860s were not a peak for business activity as they were

Figure 3.12 **Business Activity in the United States** (decade averages)

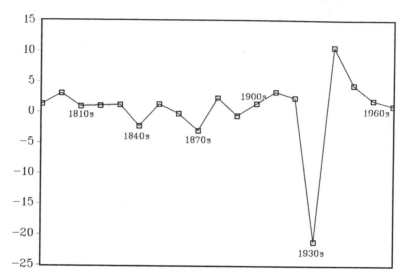

for money growth and inflation. Similarly, the 1970s were not a peak for business activity, but then, as mentioned, the 1970s were not a peak for money growth and inflation either, although Batra's chart depicts them as one. Also note that the 1900s should be a trough decade in Figure 3.12, not the 1890s.

Another question concerns the magnitude of the forecasted depression: Will it be on a par with the Great Depression of the 1930s or the Great Depression of the 1840s? Although it would be hard to argue against applying the term "depression" to the severe contraction that lasted from early 1842 through 1844, this episode was a lamb in comparison to the contraction of 1930. Figure 3.12 verifies the stark difference in magnitude between these two depressions.

Another rule, quite different from Batra's, may be derived from the same data:

> In the U.S. economy there has been at least one expansion every decade, and a major expansion every third or fifth decade in the sense that if the third decade managed to avoid a major expansion, then the fifth decade experienced a cumulative effect—an all-out boom.

As with Batra's rule, one must regard Figure 3.12 with a generous eye in order to see that this new rule holds true. The 1830s show only a minor expansion so that the fifth decade, the 1850s, shows a more pronounced peak. After this, every third decade registers a major expansion, except the 1970s. Therefore, the fifth decade, the 1990s, should experience a cumulative effect—an all-out boom.

Contradictory conclusions from the analysis of the same subject matter are not unheard of in economics. In particular, in the analysis of business cycles and forecasting, much depends upon the eye of the beholder.

## Summary

Whatever one may think about Professor Batra's ideas, his work certainly has not raised the stature of wave theory in the forecasting profession. Nothing short of a major depression in the remaining years of the 1990s could vindicate his analysis. Such an event would also rekindle interest in the Kondratieff cycle. That cycle is hypothesized to be in a down phase since 1973. The long and exuberant expansion of the 1980s mars the dating of Kondratieff's downswing. Only a severe depression could mitigate against those gains to result in low growth for the entire 1973–1990s period.

If that great depression does not materialize, wave theorists could, of course, fall back on some exogenous shock (the crumbling of communism comes to mind) to explain the interrupted pattern.

## Notes

1. See Kitchin (1923).
2. See Juglar (1966).
3. These irregularities are sometimes attributed to the Kitchin cycle. They also may be the result of economic policies, institutional changes, or other exogenous events.
4. See Kuznets (1953).
5. Rostow (1975) is able to discern Kuznets's cycles from 1840 to 1914 in the United States, and suspects they no longer exist.
6. Schumpeter's (1939) work predates Kuznets's (1953), and thus his scheme does not include a Kuznets cycle. Theoretically, at least, the Kuznets cycle fits quite well into the interrelationship scheme: one Kondratieff is comprised of three Kuznets, which are each comprised of two Juglars, which, in turn, consist of two Kitchins each.
7. See Kondratieff (1935).
8. See Rostow (1975).
9. See Nutter (1962), Persons (1931), Frickey (1942), and U.S. Bureau of Economic Analysis (1973).

10. This data series was discontinued in 1986. Since it relied heavily on the Federal Reserve Board's index of industrial production after 1919, it is a simple matter to splice new data to the older series. The graph of the data series with labels for the prominent peaks and troughs is a favorite of economic authors. See Batra (1987, pp. 109–111) and Mansfield and Behravesh (1995, pp. 82–83) for reproductions.

11. See Reijnders (1990, pp. 11–12).

12. See ibid., p. 20.

13. See Kondratieff (1984). The original was written in 1928, but an English translation was not available until this one in 1984. In a similar fashion, Kondratieff's original explication of the long wave in 1927 did not become available in English until 1935.

14. See Van Duijn (1983, pp. 176–79) for such a list and sources of others.

15. The quotes are from Van Duijn (1983, pp. 198–99).

## References

Batra, Ravi. 1987. *The Great Depression of 1990.* New York: Simon and Schuster.

Frickey, Edwin. 1942. *Economic Fluctuations in the United States.* New York: Russell and Russell.

Juglar, Clement. 1966. *A Brief History of Panics and Their Periodical Occurrence in the United States.* New York: A.M. Kelly.

Kitchin, J. 1923. "Cycles and Trends in Economic Factors." *Review of Economic Statistics,* 5: 10–16.

Kondratieff, Nikolai D. 1935. "The Long Waves in Economic Life." *Review of Economics and Statistics,* 17: 105–115.

———. 1984. *The Long Wave Cycle.* New York: Richardson and Snyder.

Kuznets, Simon. 1953. *Economic Change.* New York: W.W. Norton.

Mansfield, E., and Behravesh, N. 1995. *Economics U$A,* 4th ed. New York: W.W. Norton.

Nutter, G. Warren. 1962. *Growth of Industrial Production in the Soviet Union.* Princeton, NJ: Princeton University Press.

Persons, W.M. 1931. *Forecasting Business Cycles.* New York: John Wiley. Boston, MA: Houghton-Mifflin.

Reijnders, Jan. 1990. *Long Waves in Economic Development.* Brookfield, VT: Edward Elgar.

Rostow, W.W. 1975. "Kondratieff, Schumpeter, and Kuznets: Trend Periods Revisited." *Journal of Economic History,* 35: 719–53.

Schumpeter, Joseph. 1927. "The Explanation of the Business Cycle." *Economica* (December): 286–311.

———. 1939. *Business Cycles,* vols. 1 and 2. New York: McGraw-Hill.

U.S. Bureau of Economic Analysis. 1973. *Long Term Economic Growth 1860–1970.* Washington, DC: U.S. Department of Commerce.

Van Duijn, Jacob J. 1983. *The Long Wave in Economic Life.* London: George Allen and Unwin.

# 4

# Forecasting with Economic Indicators

Wall Street indexes predicted nine of the last five recessions.

—Paul Samuelson, 1966

For over fifty years, experts and novices, learned scholars and naive upstarts have searched for statistics that signal future changes in economic activity. This chapter summarizes and evaluates those efforts. It is somewhat unfair, but nonetheless possible, to assess in a phrase or two the voluminous work in this area: some good statistical indicators have been uncovered but none of them is infallible and many are unreliable.[1]

Indeed, the efficacy of statistical indicators in forecasting future economic activity is quite controversial. It has been observed that the perfect indicator can never be found even if it does exist. The government and other decision makers would track the statistic and take offsetting policy actions that would preclude the forecasted change from coming about.[2] One might question the ability of decision makers, especially the government, to adopt and implement precisely offsetting policies. And even on a theoretical basis, the perfect indicator could be expected to have a self-fulfilling character. A rise in such an indicator would promote business and consumer optimism and, thus, economic prosperity.

But all of this is neither here nor there, since the hypothesized statistic has not been discovered. Or perhaps it has, and the discoverer is amassing a fortune by playing the financial markets (as quietly as possible) with the advantage of knowing for certain the state of the economy six months hence.[3]

## The Indicators of the U.S. Department of Commerce

### *Description*

The most widely known economic indicators are those of the Commerce Department's Bureau of Economic Analysis. At present the Bureau's series of leading economic indicators (LEIs) is comprised of eleven time series that swing up or down approximately six to twelve months before overall economic activity. Phenomena such as the stock market, the money supply, and average hours worked per week tend to fluctuate prior to general business activity.

The eleven separate series can be combined into one statistic known as the composite index of leading economic indicators (series no. 910). The calculation of this composite index is a bit cumbersome. Basically, a weighted average of the eleven data series is taken where the weights are based on the reliability of the individual series.[4] The composite index of LEIs attracts quite a bit of media attention upon its release each month. Financial markets sometimes react to the economic forecast implicit in this number, especially when the released figure is surprisingly high or low.

As Table 4.1 shows, the composite index of the LEIs turns down on average 11.6 months before overall economic activity. But the same index turned down twenty months before the August 1957 recession and five months before the recession of 1953. During a recession, the LEIs typically turn up 3.1 months before the expansion begins. The lead time for signaling expansions, however, has been as long as ten months and as short as one month. The problem posed by this lead-time variability is discussed below.

The composite index of the LEIs is an index number. This means that its value was arbitrarily set equal to 100 in the base time period—1987. If the composite index reads 102 today, this means the index is 2 percent higher than its average reading in 1987. The changes in the composite index of the LEIs are considered important gauges of future economic activity. A large increase (greater than 0.5 percent) is indicative of an improving economic climate. Three consecutive declines mean a recession within the next twelve months. The reliability of rules such as these is considered shortly.

The Bureau of Economic Analysis also compiles and updates a monthly series of four coincident economic indicators (CEIs) (see

Table 4.1

**The Leading Indicators**

| Series no. | Series title | Average lead time (months) signaling recessions | Average lead time (months) signaling expansions |
|---|---|---|---|
| 1 | Average weekly hours, mfg. | 11.0 | 1.2 |
| 5 | Average weekly initial claims for unemployment insurance[a] | 12.9 | 0.1 |
| 8 | Manufacturers' new orders, consumer goods and materials[b] | 9.3 | 1.8 |
| 32 | Vendor performance, slower deliveries, diffusion index | 8.4 | 4.2 |
| 20 | Contracts and orders for plant and equipment[b] | 7.3 | 0.0 |
| 29 | Building permits, new private housing units | 15.4 | 5.4 |
| 92 | Change in manufacturers' unfilled orders, durable goods[b,c] | 10.6 | 0.6 |
| 99 | Change in sensitive materials prices[c] | 7.9 | 1.7 |
| 19 | Index of stock prices, 500 common stocks | 11.1 | 4.6 |
| 106 | Money supply, M2[b] | 14.2 | 5.2 |
| 83 | Index of consumer expectations | 12.4 | 4.0 |
| 910 | Composite index of 11 leading indicators | 11.6 | 3.1 |

*Source*: U.S. Department of Commerce.

[a]This series is inverted—that is, low values are peaks and high values are troughs.

[b]This series is adjusted for price changes.

[c]This series is smoothed by an autoregressive-moving-average filter developed by Statistics Canada.

Table 4.2). As the name suggests, these statistics swing in tandem with the business cycle. Taken together, the CEIs are a good measure of what the LEIs are purported to forecast.

There is also an index of lagging economic indicators (LgEIs) (Table 4.3). These eight data series turn up or down after overall activity. The LgEIs are useful for confirming movements in the LEIs, the CEIs, and the business cycle. Moreover, the ratio of the composite index of the CEIs to the composite index of the LgEIs is considered to be a leading economic indicator (series no. 940).

The ratio index has a slightly shorter average lead time than the

Table 4.2

## The Coincident Indicators

| Series no. | Series title |
|---|---|
| 41 | Employees on nonagricultural payrolls |
| 51 | Personal income less transfer payments[a] |
| 47 | Index of industrial production |
| 57 | Manufacturing and trade sales[a] |
| 920 | Composite index of four coincident indicators |

*Source*: U.S. Department of Commerce.
[a]This series is adjusted for price changes.

Table 4.3

## The Lagging Indicators

| Series no. | Series title | Average lag time signaling recessions (months) | Average lag time signaling expansions (months) |
|---|---|---|---|
| 91 | Average duration of unemployment[a] | 0.0 | 10.6 |
| 77 | Ratio, manufacturing and trade inventories to sales[b] | 9.2 | 17.4 |
| 62 | Change in index of labor cost per unit of output[c] | 6.4 | 9.7 |
| 109 | Average prime rate charged by banks | 2.0 | 17.9 |
| 101 | Commercial and industrial loans outstanding[b] | 4.6 | 8.3 |
| 95 | Ratio, consumer installment credit to personal income | 1.0 | 6.6 |
| 120 | Change in consumer price index for services[c] | 1.9 | 8.3 |
| 930 | Composite index of seven lagging indicators | 3.1 | 9.3 |

*Source*: U.S. Department of Commerce.
[a]This series is inverted—low values are peaks and high values are troughs.
[b]This series is adjusted for price changes.
[c]This series is smoothed by an autoregressive-moving-average filter developed by Statistics Canada.

LEIs in signaling recessions and recoveries, but in many instances it has signaled first. Considering all these indicators, one may wonder why forecasters have such a difficult time of it.

Figure 4.1 **Composite Index of Leading Economic Indicators**

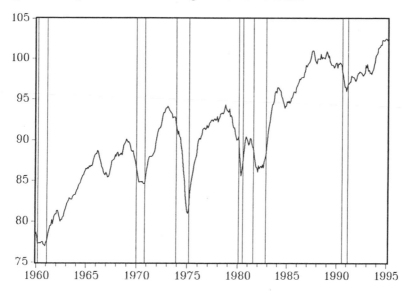

## Evaluation

Do changes in the composite index of the LEIs foretell changes in economic activity? Yes. But that response needs to be qualified. First, the lead time given by the composite index varies rather widely. On average, the index turns down eleven months before a contraction and turns up three months before an expansion begins. Yet, the composite index of the LEIs turned down only five months before the 1953 recession. The composite index turned up just one month before the expansion which began in March 1975 (see Figure 4.1). In this case, it might be said that no advance warning of the upcoming expansion was provided at all, considering that the figures are released with a one-month lag. Even then, the figures comprising the LEIs are subject to revision.

Even if we concede that the LEIs do a fairly good job of predicting impending turns in economic activity, they do not provide forecasts of the exact dates of those turns. Furthermore, the forecasts are not quantitative. That is, they do not provide numerical predictions for specific variables such as GDP, employment, and interest rates. The LEIs merely attempt to discern, in advance, a change in the general eco-

Table 4.4

**Major Stock Market Drops**

| Stock market downturn | Decline in Dow Jones Industrial Average (percent) | Start of recession |
|---|---|---|
| Jun. 17, 1901, to Nov. 9, 1903 | 46.1 | Sep. 1902 |
| Jan. 19, 1906, to Nov. 15, 1907 | 48.5 | May 1907 |
| Nov. 21, 1916, to Dec. 19, 1917 | 40.1 | Aug. 1918 |
| Nov. 3, 1919, to Aug. 24, 1921 | 46.6 | Jan. 1920 |
| Sep. 3, 1929, to Jul. 8, 1932 | 89.2 | Aug. 1929 |
| Mar. 10, 1937, to Mar. 31, 1938 | 49.1 | May 1937 |
| Nov. 12, 1938, to Apr. 28, 1942 | 41.3 | — |
| Dec. 3, 1968, to May 26, 1970 | 35.9 | Dec. 1969 |
| Jan. 11, 1973, to Dec. 6, 1974 | 45.1 | Nov. 1973 |
| Aug. 25, 1987, to Oct. 19, 1987 | 36.1 | — |

*Source: The Wall Street Journal.*

nomic climate. It has been suggested that more quantitative forecasting techniques do not detect these turning points as well as the LEIs.[5]

Often, turning points are not signaled all that clearly. For instance, coming up to the recession that began in November 1973, the LEIs flashed hot and cold, and ended up increasing the month the recession began. The opposite problem, a clear but false signal, occurs with some frequency. In the middle of 1984, sixteen months into a recovery, the composite index turned down and continued to decline each month for six months. No recession materialized.[6]

The deficiencies of indicator forecasting are made evident by examining the postwar record of one of the best-known components of the composite index of LEIs: stock prices. Standard and Poor's index of 500 common stock prices has sent false signals (1987), no-calls (1980), and provided a wide range of lead times (zero to thirty months) before recessions. The record for predicting expansions is similarly spotty. But the focus here is on contractions, since declines in the stock market, especially large declines, are widely believed to predate recessions (see Table 4.4).

Since 1900 there have been ten declines of 35 percent or more in stock prices. Two of these—1939 and 1876—were false signals.[7] The largest percentage decline in Standard and Poor's index began late in 1929, but the NBER Business Cycle Dating Committee sets the start of

Figure 4.2 **Ratio Index, LEIs/CEIs**

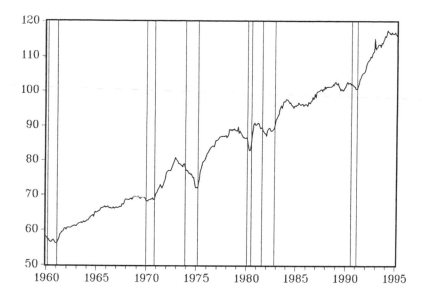

the Great Depression in August 1929. There is not much lead time there, or in the subsequent recession beginning in May 1937. Stock prices began their 50 percent descent two months earlier. On the other hand, in two cases (1907 and 1969) the lead times were long enough (sixteen months and twelve months, respectively) to make one wonder if the market decline and subsequent recession were actually associated.

There is a theoretical explanation for the association between stock prices and future economic activity. The idea is that stock market participants foresee—indeed, are rewarded for foreseeing—imminent changes in the economic climate. The more successfully future developments are incorporated into today's stock prices, the more strongly the two are related. In a similar fashion, theoretical connections between each of the eleven LEIs and the future state of the economy can be made. But the search for and development of economic indicators generally has been devoid of theory.[8]

The ratio index, as mentioned earlier, has a slightly shorter average lead time than the composite index of LEIs in signaling recessions: 11.2 months compared with 11.6 months (see Figure 4.2). Increases in the ratio index during contractions precede the onset of the recovery by an average of only 2.9 months. This is slightly worse than the 3.1-

month average lead given by the composite LEIs. Again, considering the time lag before the data become available and the subsequent revisions, the lead time for both the composite LEIs and the ratio index in predicting recoveries is virtually nil.

To get a flavor of indicator forecasting, try the following test: It is the last business day in June 19- -, and the economy has been in an expansion for over two years. The figures for the composite LEIs and the ratio index for May have just been released. Those figures and the data for the previous twelve months are:

| Month | Composite LEIs | Ratio Index |
|---|---|---|
| May | 104.3 | 113.9 |
| June | 104.5 | 113.8 |
| July | 104.6 | 113.3 |
| August | 105.0 | 113.3 |
| September | 106.1 | 113.0 |
| October | 107.1 | 113.7 |
| November | 106.3 | 112.6 |
| December | 105.4 | 112.8 |
| January | 105.3 | 111.8 |
| February | 105.5 | 111.6 |
| March | 106.1 | 113.4 |
| April | 104.5 | 109.0 |
| May | 105.1 | 110.2 |

Will there be a recession within the next year? Remember, the composite index of the LEIs and the ratio index both have an average lead time of eleven months for predating recessions. Notice that specifics on what will happen to GDP, industrial production, interest rates, or other macroeconomic variables are not required. Neither is the exact date of the onset of the recession (if you think these figures suggest a recession is impending). In fact, one has a fifty-fifty chance of answering the question correctly by flipping a coin. But don't do that, since the lesson, that indicators typically send ambiguous signals that are difficult to interpret, will be lost on you. The answer to the test appears in this note.[9]

## Statistical Indicators and Prediction Rules

No forecaster would translate a one-month decline in any of the statistical indicators into a prediction of a forthcoming recession. Intermittent one-month disruptions in the normal progression of any given statistical indicator are common. These are not considered to be false signals—merely aberrations. A substantial or continual decline is necessary to infer that a slump in economic activity is impending.

This raises the question about what constitutes a substantial change in a statistical indicator. What exactly is required to interpret that an indicator is signaling a turning point in the business cycle? A good rule will cut down on the number of false signals issued by the indicator while preserving its ability to call most of the turning points.

### Hymans's Analysis

An early example of an effort to develop a decision rule to use in conjunction with economic indicators was Saul Hymans's (1973) study. Essentially, Hymans's rule stated that the composite index of the LEIs forecasted a recession when it declined for two consecutive months. During a recession, if the LEIs increased for two consecutive months, an expansion was expected. Applying this rule to the data from 1948 to 1971, he found that it failed to call the 1957 recession and gave twenty-eight false signals for recessions. The rule performed somewhat better in predicting the onset of recoveries, but provided hardly any lead time. Hymans's conclusion:

> [The LEIs] by no means performed so well as to confirm that a reliable cyclical indicator was in hand. (Hymans, 1973, p. 358)

### Anderson and Erceg's Analysis

In a more recent study, Anderson and Erceg (1989) scoured the postwar U.S. data to discover which rules would provide optimal turning point signals. Their goal was to determine the number of monthly declines in the LEIs that would signal recessions while avoiding false signals and no-calls, and still provide ample, but not excessive, warning. The same exercise was performed to determine the best rule for predicting expansions.

They found that the optimal signal to warn of a forthcoming recession is when the LEIs decline four out of the previous seven months. This rule generated four false signals but never failed to foresee an oncoming cyclical peak. The lead time given by this forecasting rule, however, varies greatly—from one to fourteen months. Thus, if the composite index of the LEIs declines four out of seven months, chances are two out of three that a recession will begin sometime in the next fourteen months.

During a recession, the best rule Anderson and Erceg found to predict an impending recovery was if the LEIs rise for two consecutive months. This is the same rule Hymans tested. In the postwar period, this rule incorrectly gave advance notice of a recovery twice and failed to provide any indication of two of the recoveries. The lead times of these warnings varied from one to nine months. Hence, if the composite index of the LEIs rises for two consecutive months during a recession, chances are three to one that a recovery will commence within nine months.

Anderson and Erceg conclude:

> [The composite index of the LEIs] can provide useful information, but its value as a forecasting tool is quite limited. (Anderson and Erceg, 1989, p. 7)

The performance of Anderson and Erceg's rules can be improved slightly if they are used in conjunction with the ratio index. For instance, if it is stipulated that both the LEIs and the ratio index must meet the four-out-of-seven rule to provide a valid signal for a recession, then only three false signals are given in the postwar era and the variability of the lead time range narrows to one to nine months.

### Zarnowitz and Moore's Analysis

Zarnowitz and Moore (1983) considered a variety of rules to be used in conjunction with the LEIs and the CEIs to predict business-cycle turning points more effectively. These authors preferred to work not with the raw data concerning the LEIs and the CEIs, but with the "smoothed" data. Smoothing the data consists of "taking the ratio of the current month's index to the average of the twelve preceding months and expressing the resulting percentage at an annual compound rate" (Zarnowitz and Moore, 1983, p. 27).

The two series produced by applying the smoothing process to the LEIs and the CEIs can be used to forecast turning points in economic activity. The simplest forecast rule uses only the smoothed LEIs: when it registers above 3.3 percent (its long-run target trend), an expansion is indicated; below 3.3 percent signals a forthcoming recession.

This rule suffers from the usual indicator deficiencies: false signals, no-calls, and variable lead times. The alternate rules considered by Zarnowitz and Moore remedy one or two of these deficiencies while exacerbating the other(s). As an example, the recession rule can be modified to say that the LEIs must become negative and the CEIs must fall below 3.3 percent. This will reduce the number of false signals, but it also increases the number of no-calls and drastically reduces the average lead time.

## Diffusion Indexes

A large number of data series simultaneously changing their direction—going from increasing to decreasing or vice versa—could imply that a change in the economic climate is in the offing. This is the basic idea behind diffusion indexes. There are several sorts of diffusion indexes, some of which are not explicitly intended to forecast future economic activity. In chapter 2, the degree to which a recession is dispersed throughout the economy was measured with a diffusion index: the percentage of industries with falling employment levels. Of the diffusion indexes that are commonly used for forecasting, those of the Department of Commerce are most widely regarded.

### Diffusion Indexes of the Bureau of Economic Analysis

The Commerce Department's Bureau of Economic Analysis is able to form a diffusion index from the eleven LEIs.[10] In any month, this diffusion index is equal to the percentage of the eleven data series that have risen over a given time span. The standard time spans considered are one and six months.

To be more specific, let us consider the formation of the diffusion index of the eleven LEIs over a one-month span (see Figure 4.3). A data series that has risen compared with the previous month gets a score of "1."[11] Scores of "0" are assigned to series that have decreased, and "0.5" to series that have remained unchanged. Notice that the magnitudes of the increases or decreases in any given series are not taken into account. If a series declines, it receives a score of "0" regardless of the magnitude of that decline. The scores are totaled and divided by eleven.

This sort of diffusion index can display erratic behavior if the indi-

Figure 4.3 **Diffusion Index of the LEIs** (one-month span)

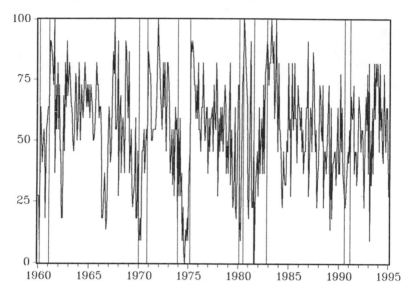

vidual series are continually bobbing up and down around a long-term trend. To overcome this problem, diffusion indexes can be calculated over a longer time span. To calculate the six-month diffusion index of the LEIs, the scoring is the same as with the one-month index (see Figure 4.4). Now, however, the series scores a "1" if it has risen from its value three months earlier when compared with its value two months after the current month. Thus, it is said that a six-month diffusion index is "centered" on the fourth month. This centering scheme implies an additional two-month delay in availability. The six-month diffusion index of the LEIs is not as erratic as the one-month index, but suffers from the usual indicator deficiencies.

Renshaw (1991) has outlined a useful approach to forecasting with the one-month diffusion index. Based on the idea that economic growth is three-tiered, one can predict the growth rate for real GNP over the next year according to the following rule:

> By simply setting the predicted growth rate for real GNP equal to –1.0 percent when the diffusion index for the [LEIs] had an average value less than 46 percent; 2.9 percent when the value for the diffusion index was in the 46–60 percent range; 5.4 percent when the diffusion index had an average value over 60 percent. (Renshaw, 1991, p. 200)

Figure 4.4 **Diffusion Index of the LEIs** (six-month span)

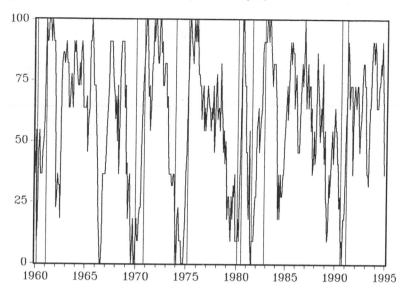

Renshaw noted that these predictions may have to be lowered, given the recent tendency toward slower economic growth. Reapplying Renshaw's technique to real GDP growth for the 1960–90 period results in the following rule: predict –0.8 percent growth for real GDP over the next year when the diffusion index of the LEIs (one-month span) averages 46 percent or less for the current year; predict 2.6 percent growth when the diffusion index averages between 46 percent and 60 percent; and predict 5.1 percent growth when the diffusion index averages 60 percent or more.

Although this simple technique performs surprisingly well, it is far from perfect. For instance, although this approach correctly predicted all the negative growth periods in the postwar era, it also forecasted negative growth in four cases that never materialized (1952, 1957, 1961, and 1967). In order to cut down on false signals such as these, Renshaw advocates using his rule in conjunction with other forecasting procedures.[12]

### The Diffusion Index of Employment Gains

The Department of Commerce creates another diffusion index by monitoring the number of industries that are experiencing gains in employment.[13] All together, 356 industries are observed. The number of these industries that have registered gains in employment over the previous month is divided by 356. The resulting fraction gives the percentage of industries experiencing rising employment.

The diffusion index of employment gains is an excellent gauge of the dispersion of economic growth. If the economy is in the midst of an expansion but less than 70 percent of the industries are registering job growth, then it can be said that the expansion is not broad-based. The brief recovery from July 1980 to July 1981 was narrow in scope. The maximum percentage of industries displaying job growth during that episode peaked at 70.9 percent.

In a similar fashion, the diffusion index of employment gains can monitor how widespread a recession is throughout the economy. If 35 percent or more of the industries are experiencing job growth during the recession, then the slow-down is not very dispersed. This was the case in the contraction that began in January 1980 and ended six months later. In its worst month, 37.1 percent of the industries across the economy were still showing job growth.

The diffusion index of employment growth does more than just gauge the dispersion of recessions and recoveries. It can be a signal of change in the economic climate. If the diffusion index of employment gains displays an abrupt change in either direction, this can be an indication of an impending change in the business cycle. Figure 4.5 shows the cyclical nature of the employment gains diffusion index. During recessions, far fewer industries register employment gains. Notice that the index has a tendency to swing suddenly as the economy moves from one phase of the business cycle to another.

It is also evident in Figure 4.5 that the diffusion index of employment gains is highly erratic. Because of this, some analysts prefer to consider the same index based on a six-month span. As explained in the previous section, the six-month spanning procedure takes some of the volatility out of the time series. But it also adds two months to the time the current figure becomes available.

## More Exotic Statistical Indicators

As we have seen, forecasting with garden-variety statistical indicators is fraught with pitfalls. Thus, the search for a superior indicator continues. These continuing efforts have produced several more sophisti-

Figure 4.5 **Diffusion Index of Industries Showing Employment Gains**

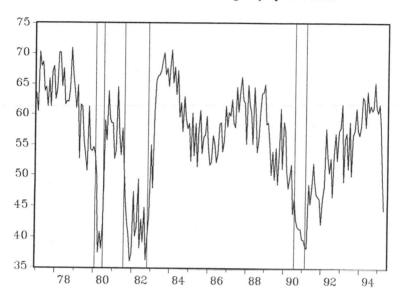

cated (which does not necessarily imply better) but less-known indicators. This section discusses some of these less-established techniques
in indicator forecasting.

### Long- and Short-Leading Indicators

Geoffrey Moore, one of the pioneers of indicator forecasting, is still
hard at work refining previous efforts and developing new indicators
(Moore, 1990). As the director of the Center for International Business
Cycle Research (CIBCR) at Columbia University, he has made suggestions for improving the standard economic indicators of the Bureau
of Economic Analysis. Some of those suggestions were adopted in the
1989 revision of those indicators. Moore has also proposed a new set
of indicators: the long-leading and short-leading indexes.

To be included in the long-leading indicators, a data series must lead
downturns in economic activity by at least twelve months on average,
and must lead upturns by six months. Two of the eleven LEIs make the
grade: the money supply and building permits. An index of bond prices
and the ratio of price to unit labor cost in manufacturing also have been
found to meet the stipulated lead times. A composite index can be

Table 4.5

**Components of the Long-Leading Index of the Center for International Business Cycle Research**

| Series name | Average lead time signaling recessions (months) | Average lead time signaling expansions (months) |
|---|---|---|
| Dow Jones Index of bond prices | 27 | 7 |
| Ratio, price/unit labor cost, manufacturing | 26 | 6 |
| Money supply, M2[a] | 17 | 6 |
| Building permits, new private housing | 15 | 6 |

*Source*: Center for International Business Cycle Research.
[a]This series is adjusted for price changes.

formed from these four components and it is this composite index that has taken the name "long-leading index." As with all statistical indicators, an economic rationale for the leading behavior of each of the four series that constitute the long-leading index can be made. However, statistical reliability is the most important criterion for inclusion on the list (see Table 4.5).

The long-leading index, shown in Figure 4.6, gave advance warning of each recession and revival, but the lead times of these signals varied widely enough to diminish their usefulness. For recessions, the lead times ranged from seven to twenty-seven months. Thus, a sustained decline in the long-leaders implies a forthcoming contraction in business activity. However, that recession may commence in half a year or in two years. This is not precise enough even for qualitative forecasting. The long-leaders have also incorrectly signaled recessions in 1951 and 1966.[14]

As for signaling recoveries, the long-leading index, on average, gave advance notice of eight months. Again, the lead times of those notices varied widely—from two to fifteen months. There were no false signals of recoveries, but a case can be made that there were some unclear signals. Specifically, the recoveries from the recessions in 1960 and 1970 were not clearly indicated.

The short-leading index is composed of eleven component series (see Table 4.6). Five of these are from the LEIs: stock prices, average work week in manufacturing, initial claims for unemployment insurance, new orders for consumer goods and materials, and contracts and orders for plant and equipment. The remaining six series have been

Figure 4.6 **Long-Leading Index of the CIBCR**

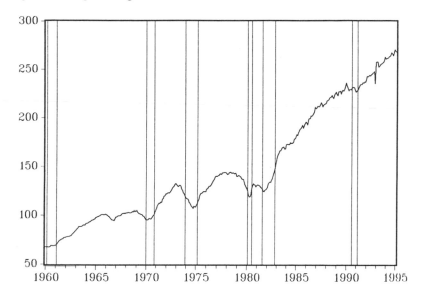

Table 4.6

**Components of the Short-Leading Index of the Center for International Business Cycle Research**

| Series name | Average lead time signaling recessions (months) | Average lead time signaling expansions (months) |
|---|---|---|
| Change in nonfinancial debt[a] | 17 | 2 |
| Stock price index, S&P 500 | 9 | 5 |
| Average work week, manufacturing | 10 | 2 |
| Layoff rate under five weeks | 10 | 2 |
| Initial claims, unemployment insurance | 13 | 0 |
| New orders, consumer goods and materials | 8 | 4 |
| NAPM vendor performance | 8 | 5 |
| NAPM inventory change | 8 | 2 |
| Change in material prices | 8 | 2 |
| Change in business population | 9 | 2 |
| Contacts and orders for plant & equipment | 6 | 1 |

*Source*: Center for International Business Cycle Research
[a]This series is adjusted for price changes.

Figure 4.7 **Short-Leading Index of the CIBCR**

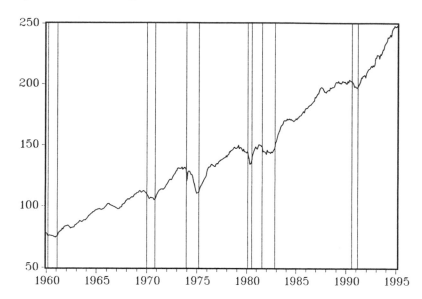

suggested for inclusion in the LEIs by CIBCR. Two of the series in the short-leading indicators come from the National Association of Purchasing Managers (NAPM). These two series are described later in this chapter. Declines in the composite index of short-leaders precede slow-downs in economic activity by eight months on average and recoveries by two months.

Like the long-leaders, the short-leading index did not miss calling a recession or a recovery. However, our weary refrain concerning false signals and variable lead times must be repeated for the short-leaders. False signals of recessions occurred in 1951 and 1966, while lead times varied from three to twenty-one months. Advance notice of revivals varied from zero to five months (see Figure 4.7).

The long-leaders and the short-leaders may be used together to signal and confirm expected turning points in the business cycle. The short-leading index typically signals six months after the long-leaders before both expansions and contractions. In a typical scenario, the long-leading index would signal an impending recession fourteen months in advance. Six months after that signal, the short-leaders would confirm or refute it. This provides eight months' advance warning before a recession.

Figure 4.8 **An Unclear Signal?**

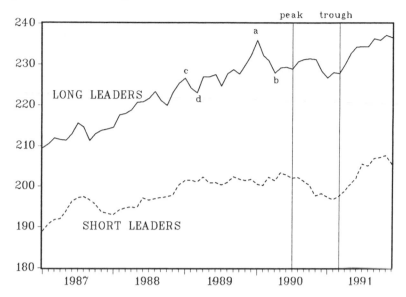

The combined signaling process prior to an expansion is similar, except the typical lead time is cut substantially. The long-leading index would signal the upcoming recovery eight months in advance and the short-leaders would confirm six months later. That leaves two months before the predicted recovery. In practice, these two months are taken up by data lags. CIBCR has experimented with indexes that only include promptly available data series in order to shorten the data lag, but so far the shortened data lag has come at the expense of shortened lead times.

Figure 4.8 illustrates the difficulty of forecasting with any indicator, and the long- and short-leading indexes in particular. At first glance it appears as if the long- and short-leaders clearly signaled the recession that began in July 1990. The long-leaders peaked in January 1990 (point a) and declined 3.43 percent in the subsequent three months (point b). However, the long-leaders then rose for several months, increasing the month the recession began. Moreover, the drop of 3.43 percent just prior to the recession is not of remarkable magnitude. In 1989, for example, the long-leaders declined 1.59 percent (points c–d). Since declines of 1 percent to 2 percent typically occur without subsequent recessions, it would have been March 1990 when the plunge from point a to point b surpassed normal dimensions. The revised data for March 1990 would have become available at the end of May, thirty days before the recession began. Of course, no one knew the recession had begun in July 1990. The NBER Business Cycle Dating Committee would not declare the official starting date until much later. Standing in July 1990 or several months beforehand, it is not at all clear that the long-leaders definitely have signaled a recession.

If one agrees that the long-leaders have ambiguously announced the 1990 recession, then little need be said about the short-leaders. Their decline began two months before the start date of the recession, but those data would not be available until the recession had already begun. Furthermore, since the drop had just begun, it had not achieved abnormal proportions until well into the recession. Finally, notice the colossal false alarm sent by the short-leaders in the latter half of 1987.

### The Experimental Indicators of Stock and Watson

John Stock and Mark Watson have developed a set of seven leading indicators on a somewhat different basis from that of the LEIs.[15] The eleven series in the LEIs were selected *individually* based on their ability to predate fluctuations in economic activity. Stock and Watson include an indicator in their composite index only if it improves the group's predictive power. Beginning with 280 candidate series, Stock and Watson made an initial cut to fifty-five indicators. These fifty-five were eventually culled to seven. Only two of the LEIs made the grade: building permits and manufacturers' unfilled orders. In addition, Stock and Watson's indicators also include three variables that monitor interest rate movements, the value of the dollar vis-à-vis foreign currencies, and part-time employment resulting from slack demand (see Table 4.7).

In another innovation, Stock and Watson use the previous values of their indicators, not just the current month's value, to form the composite index for the current month if these lagged values improve forecast performance. Their composite index for a given month is an average of the seven individual indicators plus the past values of those indicators. The past values receive less weight than the current values in the averaging process.

Perhaps the most salient feature of Stock and Watson's composite

Table 4.7

**Components of Stock and Watson's Experimental Leading Indicators**

1. New private housing authorized, building permits
2. Manufacturers' unfilled orders, durable goods industries[a]
3. Trade-weighted nominal exchange rate between the United States and the United Kingdon, Germany, France, Italy, and Japan[a]
4. Part-time work in nonagricultural industries because of slack work[a]
5. Change in yield on constant-maturity portfolio of ten-year U.S. Treasury bonds[a]
6. Spread between interest rate on six-month corporate paper and the interest rate on six-month U.S. Treasury bills
7. Spread between the yield on constant-maturity portfolio of ten-year U.S. Treasury bonds and the yield on one-year U.S. Treasury bills

*Source*: Stock and Watson (1989).
[a]This series is smoothed.

index is how it can be interpreted. If their composite index reads 4.05, it is forecasting 4.05 percent economic growth (annual rate) over the next six months. Negative or low values of the index imply a recession or growth recession within the next half year. This is another example, along with Renshaw's technique, of indicators being used to generate quantitative forecasts.

Stock and Watson's work has received quite a bit of attention from forecasters. Their composite index has become known as the experimental index of leading indicators (see Figure 4.9).

How well have the experimental indicators performed? Despite the innovative work, it is not clear that the experimental indicators are an appreciable improvement over the traditional LEIs. Preliminary tests indicate only a marginal improvement in signaling business-cycle turning points. There have been false signals of recessions (1967, 1979) and expansions (1974, 1982) and variable lead times (zero to six months). To this point in time, no comprehensive assessment of the accuracy of the quantitative forecasts implicit in the experimental index has been done. Stock and Watson, however, report a preliminary finding that their growth rate predictions are at least positively correlated with actual, future economic growth.[16]

Stock and Watson have also developed a recession index that gives the probability of a recession occurring within the next six months. This recession index is constructed with their seven leading indicators and the four coincident indicators that they have developed.[17] A reces-

Figure 4.9 **Experimental Index of Leading Economic Indicators — Historical Values since 1961**

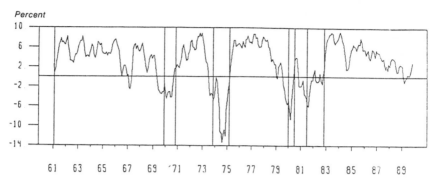

sion index that reads 0.41 is interpreted to mean that there is a 41 percent chance of a recession in the next six months. The recession index, like the experimental index, provided a false signal in 1967 and unclear signals before the 1980 and 1981 recessions. Stock and Watson's own assessment from an in-period analysis is that their recession index is 50 percent correlated with actual recessions six months hence. This correlation becomes stronger as the lead time is cut, so that the recession index is 88 percent correlated with actual recessions that are concurrent (see Figure 4.10).

Following Stock and Watson, it is becoming more common for indicator forecasts to be couched in terms of probabilities. If the recession index gives a reading of 0.99, one would conclude that a recession is virtually certain to occur within the next six months. If that recession does not come about, the recession index would have given a false signal. But, more properly, the index reading of 0.99 allows for the possibility, albeit small, that no recession would occur. In this sense, no false alarm was sounded—it just happened to be the one time in a hundred when a recession did not materialize under the circumstances. With this interpretation, Stock and Watson's recession index should always lie between zero and one and never attain those extremes, since no one can say with complete certainty whether a recession will or will not occur in the next six months. Because of the manner in which it is calculated, Stock and Watson's recession index has, in practice, been equal to zero or one.[18]

Figure 4.10 **Experimental Recession Index—Historical Values Since 1961**

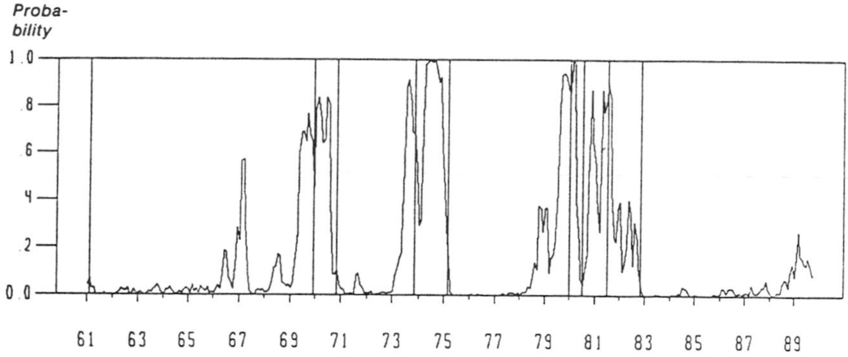

## Neftci's Contribution

Salih Neftci has developed a rule to be used in conjunction with the LEIs to predict cyclical downturns (Neftci, 1982). The rule is derived from a sequential probability analysis and assumes that a recession is more probable as the expansion increases in duration. The earlier in the expansion the recession signal is waved, the more chance of having given a false signal.

In application, one must first decide what probability of a false alarm is to be tolerated, say, 10 percent. Then, changes in the LEIs are interpreted (via calculations based on the theory of optimal stopping) to be indicative or not indicative of a recession. If the calculations imply a forthcoming contraction, there is a 10 percent probability it will not materialize. Thus, Neftci's procedure is a sophisticated rule for predicting recessions based on the LEIs.

The procedure suffers from several drawbacks. First, the probability of false signals must be decided in advance, and arbitrarily. And there is also the possibility of a no-call, which is inversely related to the probability of a false alarm. Also, when a recession is indicated, there is no explicit time frame for when it might materialize.

Despite these drawbacks, Neftci's work has proved seminal. Other researchers have expanded his approach to provide probabilistic predictions of forthcoming expansions and to incorporate not just the LEIs, but other indicators as well.[19]

In spite of the increased sophistication, none of these exotic indicators has significantly improved the predictive performance of indicator forecasting in general. The false signals, the unclear signals, the no-calls, and the wide-ranging lead times still plague this entire approach to forecasting business-cycle turning points.

**Miscellaneous Indicators**

Despite all the economic indicators discussed in this chapter, chances are your favorite indicator has not been mentioned at all. An acquaintance of mine swears by the amount of loose change he finds on the ground outside the local convenience store. People are more careful with their coins when times are tough. Another example of an obscure indicator is the gift wrap index. The amount of gift wrap used by department stores in New York City is monitored to forecast holiday retail sales. The reliability of these two particular indicators has not been formally tested, but that is the case with most of these miscellaneous indicators.

*Indicators of the National Association of Purchasing Management*

Since the end of World War II, the National Association of Purchasing Management (NAPM) has been surveying large corporations on a monthly basis. The survey responses are used to create several indexes that can be used for forecasting purposes. These indicators are rather well established and have been evaluated to a certain extent.[20] Nevertheless, they are classified here as miscellaneous since the data collected by NAPM duplicate information provided by government agencies. The NAPM data do not always behave the same as data collected by the government, and thus provide a useful comparison. Moreover, the NAPM survey data never have to be revised.

One question on the NAPM survey, which goes out to 300 large corporations, concerns new orders. The more new orders these corporations receive, the more economic activity expected in the near future. If over half the firms are reporting increased new orders, an expansion is indicated. A recession is expected in the near future if the index falls below 50 percent. Data on manufacturers' new orders are also collected by the Bureau of Economic Analysis and are one of the eleven components of the LEIs.

NAPM also ascertains the percentage of its respondents that are experiencing rising inventories. This data series behaves roughly the same as the change in manufacturing and trade inventories, which is compiled, again, by the Bureau of Economic Analysis. Both series are rather erratic and, thus, provide many false or unclear signals.

Two other NAPM indexes monitor buying prices (the prices paid by firms for their inputs) and vendor performance (the percentage of firms with slower deliveries). The Bureau of Economic Analysis collects two similar data series and includes them in the LEIs.

The four NAPM indexes can be formed into a composite index. As might be expected, the composite NAPM index behaves much like the composite index of the LEIs.

### Commodity Prices

The prices of commodities such as soybeans and pork bellies, and especially those of lumber and industrial metals, can indicate the future path of economic activity. Rises in these prices are associated with economic prosperity, but also with inflation. The association is easily explained: as the economy heats up, more of these commodities are demanded, raising their prices. Even more useful are the prices of commodities in futures markets. Since these markets speculate upon the future prices of the commodities, they necessarily take into account the future levels of demand and economic activity. The Commodity Research Bureau promulgates several of these sorts of indexes. The best known of these is commonly referred to as the CRB and reflects the prices of a bundle of commodities in the futures market.

A favorite indicator with many forecasters is scrap metal prices, or, as they are affectionately known, scraps. Scrap prices seem to be especially sensitive to industrial demand, especially domestic industrial demand. The drawback to using scrap prices is that they provide little, if any, lead time.

Although many forecasters consider commodity prices in their analyses, they use them with caution. Commodity prices have a reputation for giving false signals.

### Housing Starts

Private housing starts are often a useful economic indicator. The number of housing starts can be a reflection of a variety of economic factors. Aside from demographic trends, housing starts are affected by income, consumer confidence, interest rates, and expected inflation. The interaction and simultaneous movement of all of these factors can complicate the interpretation of housing start data.

The Bureau of Economic Analysis also collects information on housing starts by looking at the number of building permits issued by local authorities. This data series is one of the eleven LEIs.

### Help Wanted Advertising

An index of help wanted advertising is another economic indicator. The Conference Board forms an index from the amount of help wanted advertising found in fifty-one newspapers across the nation. Increases in help wanted advertising can indicate future increases in employment and income. In practice, help wanted advertising gives an average of eight months' advance notice before a recession, but lags behind at the beginning of expansions. Help wanted data tend to swing widely and often without subsequent changes in employment. Another drawback to this indicator is that structural changes in the labor market affect its behavior. For instance, the increased prevalence of firms that provide temporary help has tended to lower the amount of help wanted advertising. These declines have no significance in regard to future economic activity.

### Inflation Indicators

Finally, a variety of indicators are considered to be helpful in forecasting the future rate of inflation. Commodity prices are often used for this purpose. So are indexes of unit labor costs, producer prices, and raw materials prices. P-star is an inflation indicator developed by the Federal Reserve System. All of these are mentioned to demonstrate that the discussion of economic indicators in this chapter is by no means comprehensive. The reader is encouraged to explore the field further and in more detail.[21]

### Summary

This chapter has shown that the perfect economic indicator does not exist. None of the indicators, regardless of the sophistication that went into their design and development, is infallible. Most suffer from the problems of variable lead times, false signals, no-calls, and unclear signals. Decision rules can help alleviate these drawbacks to some extent, but these rules are far from perfect.

Yet some good statistical indicators have been uncovered. Only a very few respected forecasters would want to make their forecasts without considering at least some of these indicators. But using economic statistics well requires skill. The trick is to understand the drawbacks and limitations of the indicators at hand and to rely on them accordingly. Continuing research and development undoubtedly will improve the performance of this sort of forecasting.

## Notes

1. Mitchell and Burns (1938) and Moore (1950) were the pioneers in the search for economic indicators. Moore is still at it (Moore and Lahiri, 1991).

2. Economic forecasters have used this idea to explain unfulfilled predictions over the years. See Epstein (1987, pp. 194–95).

3. As Wall Street aficionados understand, knowledge of the state of the economy six months hence is an edge, but not a guarantee, to successful investments.

4. See the *Handbook of Cyclical Indicators* (1984) for the details concerning the calculation of the composite index.

5. See Stekler (1991, p. 169).

6. Proponents of the indicator approach note that economic activity slowed substantially starting in the second quarter of 1986. But this would imply a lead time of almost two years.

7. The onset of World War II might be used to explain why no recession followed the 1939 drop in the stock market.

8. The criticism that economic indicators lack theoretical underpinning goes back to Koopmans (1947). A formal framework for interpreting the values of economic indicators at any given time is also lacking. De Leeuw (1991) addresses this issue.

9. Yes, a recession does occur within the next year. It is June 1979 and the recession begins in seven months: January 1980.

10. Diffusion indexes are also formed for the coincident and lagging indicators, although these are not widely used for forecasting. Would the ratio of the diffusion index of the coincident indicators to the diffusion index of the lagging indicators have any predictive power, as does the ratio index (which is the ratio of the coincident indicators to the lagging indicators)?

11. Except for initial claims for unemployment insurance. Since a rise in this series is unfavorable, it scores a "1" when it declines. Also, this series must be "inverted" before it is included with the others to form the composite index of the LEIs.

12. Also notice that Renshaw's technique generates quantitative forecasts from a qualitative indicator (i.e., the diffusion index of the LEIs). See Moore (1969) and Broder and Stekler (1975) for other ways to generate quantitative

forecasts from the LEIs. Moore's technique is employed in chapter 8 of this book.

13. The diffusion index of employment gains is series number 963 in the Bureau of Economic Analysis' (BEA) numbering scheme. Updates of the index are published monthly along with the other economic indicators of the BEA in the *Survey of Current Business.*

14. The false signal in 1951 can be attributed to the Korean War. The war postponed the recession.

15. See Stock and Watson (1989). Stock and Watson's work also goes a long way toward addressing Koopman's criticism that economic indicators represent measurement without theory.

16. Specifically, Stock and Watson find that the correlation coefficient between their experimental index and economic growth six months later is 0.634. This correlation coefficient, however, is the result of calculations made within the sample period that generated the index.

17. Stock and Watson's four coincident indicators are very similar to the CEIs of the Bureau of Economic Analysis.

18. See Henderson and Seaman (1994) for another index that forecasts expansions and recessions in terms of probabilities.

19. See Kling (1987) and Diebold and Rudebusch (1989) for these extensions and advances.

20. See Klein and Moore (1991) for this evaluation.

21. Hildebrand (1992) and Tainer (1993) are excellent references and a good place to start a more detailed investigation.

## References

Anderson, Gerald H., and Erceg, John J. 1989. "Forecasting Turning Points with Leading Indicators." *Economic Commentary—Federal Reserve Bank of Cleveland* (October).

Broder, I., and Stekler, H.O. 1975. "Forecasting with a Deflated Index of Leading Series." *New England Economic Review* (September–October): 15–27.

Bureau of Economic Analysis, U.S. Department of Commerce. 1995. *Survey of Current Business.*

De Leeuw, Frank. 1991. "Toward a Theory of Leading Indicators." In Geoffrey H. Moore and Kajal Lahiri (eds.), *Leading Economic Indicators: New Approaches and Forecasting Records.* New York: Cambridge University Press, pp. 15–56.

Diebold, Francis X., and Rudebusch, Glenn D. 1989. "Scoring the Leading Indicators." *Journal of Business,* 62 (3): 369–91.

Epstein, Roy J. 1987. *A History of Econometrics.* Amsterdam: North-Holland.

Henderon, J.W., and Seaman, S.L. 1994. "Predicting Turning Points in Economic Activity with Indexes of Economic Indicators: Improved Reliability using a Logistic Model." *Business Economics* (January): 40–45.

Hildebrand, George. 1992. *Business Cycle Indicators and Measures.* Chicago: Probus.

Hymans, Saul H. 1973. "On the Use of Leading Indicators to Predict Cyclical Turning Points." *Brookings Papers on Economic Activity,* 2: 339–84.

Klein, Philip P., and Moore, Geoffrey H. 1991. "Purchasing Management Survey Data: Their Value as Leading Indicators." In Geoffrey H. Moore and Kajal Lahiri (eds.), *Leading Economic Indicators*. New York: Cambridge University Press, pp. 403–28.

Kling, James L. 1987. "Predicting the Turning Points of Business and Economic Time Series." *Journal of Business* (April): 201–38.

Koopmans, Tjalling C. 1947. "Measurement without Theory." *Review of Economics and Statistics* (August): 161–72.

Mitchell, C., and Burns, A. 1938. "Statistical Indicators of Cyclical Revivals." In Geoffrey Moore (ed.), *Business Cycle Indicators*. Princeton, NJ: Princeton University Press, 1961, pp. 162–83.

Moore, Geoffrey H. 1950. "Statistical Indicators of Cyclical Revivals and Recessions." In Geoffrey Moore (ed.), *Business Cycle Indicators*. Princeton, NJ: Princeton University Press, 1961, pp. 184–260.

———. 1969. "Forecasting Short-Term Economic Change." *Journal of the American Statistical Association* (March): 1–22.

———. 1990. *Leading Indicators for the 1990s*. Homewood, IL: Dow Jones–Irwin.

Moore, Geoffrey H., and Lahiri, Kajal, eds. 1991. *Leading Economic Indicators: New Approaches and Forecasting Records*. New York: Cambridge University Press.

Neftci, Salih N. 1982. "Optimal Prediction of Cyclical Downturns." *Journal of Economic Dynamics and Control* (August): 225–41.

Renshaw, Edward F. 1991. "Using a Consensus of Leading Indicators to Find the Right Ball Park for Real GNP Forecasts." In Geoffrey H. Moore and Kajal Lahiri (eds.), *Leading Economic Indicators: New Approaches and Forecasting Records*. New York: Cambridge University Press, pp. 197–209.

Steckler, H.O. 1991. "Turning Point Predictions, Errors, and Forecasting Procedures." In Geoffrey H. Moore and Kajal Lahiri (eds.), *Leading Economic Indicators: New Approaches and Forecasting Records*. New York: Cambridge University Press, pp. 169–81.

Stock, James H., and Watson, Mark W. 1989. "New Indexes of Coincident and Leading Economic Indicators." In *NBER Macroeconomics Annual*. Cambridge, MA: MIT Press, pp. 351–94.

Tainer, Evelina. 1993. *Using Economic Indicators to Improve Investment Analysis*. New York: John Wiley.

U.S. Department of Commerce. 1984. *Handbook of Cyclical Indicators*. Washington, DC: Government Printing Office.

Zarnowitz, Victor, and Moore, Geoffrey H. 1983. "Sequential Signals of Recession and Recovery." In Geoffrey H. Moore (ed.), *Business Cycles, Inflation, and Forecasting*. Cambridge, MA: Ballinger, pp. 23–59.

# 5

# Forecasting with Time-Series Techniques

A trend is a trend is a trend
But the question is, will it bend?
Will it alter its course
Through some unforeseen force,
And come to a premature end?

—Sir Alec Cairncross, 1969

Time-series techniques are forecasting procedures that rely on very little information. In fact, no information other than the past values of the data series to be forecasted is required. Because of this (and thanks to computer programs that do the heavy-duty calculations), time-series techniques are inexpensive, in terms of time and effort, to apply. But these techniques are often considered naive since readily available information is ignored. In practice, this drawback can be overcome by spicing the computer-generated forecasts with doses of judgment. The predictions of even the most sophisticated forecasting procedures are always adjusted to conform with the good sense of the forecaster. Time-series techniques are no different from any other technique in this sense.

Even unadjusted time-series predictions serve as a "straw man" with which other forecasts can be compared. It would be a major embarrassment if time-series techniques outperformed more complex and time-consuming forecasting procedures. As we shall see, time-series forecasts can compete with predictions generated by the best forecasters in the nation. Thus, the very best forecasters consider time-series analysis when making their predictions.

In the 1970s, Charles Nelson started a forecasting firm now known as Benchmark Forecast, which provides time-series forecasts on a wide array of economic variables. Today, the firm is headed by Frederick Joutz and its predictions serve as a benchmark for other forecasters. If your forecasts are not more accurate than those from a time-series technique, why are you wasting all that time and effort? And charging your clients those high fees? In fact, there is a good response to these questions, as we shall see most clearly in the next chapter: We provide our clients with economic analysis, not just numerical predictions. Time-series forecasts are based on statistical theory, not economic theory. (Some may consider this an advantage!) Therefore, the time-series forecaster has no insight into the economic forces that drive the numbers. The time-series forecaster can adjust the predictions in light of current economic events and may use economic theory to do so. Still, economic theory is not formally incorporated into the procedure.

**Trend Extrapolation**

The simplest time-series technique is trend extrapolation. Think of the businessperson presenting a chart of the corporation's profits, where the profit line eventually becomes dotted to represent the forecast. Taking the growth rate of a corporation's profits, or the growth rate of any economic variable, and extending it into the future is unlikely to yield satisfactory predictions. In the case of economic activity, we have already seen that the economy waxes and wanes in nonperiodic cycles. It does not grow steadily along a given trend.

Say it is 1979 and we extend the average growth rate of economic activity, as measured by real GDP, into the immediate future. The average annual growth rate of real GDP has been 3.41 percent since World War II. Real GDP in 1979 was $3,796.8 billion. The trend forecasts for 1980 and 1981 would then be $3,926.3 billion and $4,060.2 billion, respectively. The actual values for real GDP in 1980 and 1981 were $3,776.3 billion and $3,843.1 billion. The forecast errors, $150.0 billion and $217.1 billion, are rather large—4.0 percent and 5.6 percent, respectively. One would have done better to simply assume real GDP would not have changed from its 1979 level.

These poor forecasts are explained by the fact that the trend extrapolation procedure did not—indeed, can never—anticipate deviations from the trend. In 1980 and 1981, the U.S. economy suffered from recessions.

Table 5.1

**Actual and Trend-Forecasted Real GDP**

| Year | Real GDP | Short-range trend forecast | Short-range error | Long-range trend forecast | Long-range error |
|------|----------|----------------------------|-------------------|---------------------------|------------------|
| 1980 | 3,776.3 | 3,926.3 | −150.0 | 3,906.3 | −130.0 |
| 1981 | 3,843.1 | 4,060.2 | −217.1 | 4,042.2 | −199.1 |

The short-range forecast for 1980 is obtained by taking real GDP in 1979 (3,796.8) and multiplying by 1.0341. (Real GDP growth averaged 3.41 percent from 1946 to 1979.) The short-range forecast for 1981 is obtained by taking the forecast for 1980 (3,926.3) and multiplying by 1.0341.

The long-range forecast for 1980 is obtained by taking real GDP in 1960 (1,970.8) and multiplying by 1.0348.[20] (Real GDP growth averaged 3.48 percent from 1946 to 1960.) The long-range forecast for 1981 is obtained by taking the forecast for 1980 and multiplying by 1.0348.

The short- and long-range forecast errors are obtained by taking the actual real GDP for a given year and subtracting the forecast for that year. The negative numbers indicate that the forecasts overestimated the actual figures.

Trend extrapolation, however, can perform well when one is making long-range forecasts; over the long haul, the ups and downs of a given data series have a tendency to wash each other out. In 1960, real GDP was $1,970.8 and its average trend growth rate was 3.48 percent since 1946. This results in forecasts of $3,906.3 billion for 1980 and $4,042.2 billion for 1981. These are more accurate than the short-range forecasts, and more impressive considering that they were made twenty years earlier (see Table 5.1).

Even when one is making long-range forecasts, trend extrapolation can fail miserably if there has been a major shift in the long-run trend of a given data series. We know the major macroeconomic variables—GDP, interest rates, inflation, and the like—move in cycles. But do these phenomena bob and weave about a stationary long-term trend? Recent research, though not conclusive, has cast some doubt as to whether they do. Since it has implications for other time-series techniques as well, we consider this research later in this chapter.

Let us close this section on trend extrapolation by mentioning that the dotted line representing a firm's forecasted sales need not be straight. Trends may be extended into the future assuming dampened, asymptotic, or explosive growth. Application of the logistic function allows for an S-shaped extrapolation. The forecaster, using a priori information, must choose which of these to apply.

**Exponential Smoothing**

We have already noted that growth rates that held in the past may not prevail in the future. The dilemma over which growth rate to use when extrapolating a data series is overcome with a time-series technique known as exponential smoothing.[1] This technique considers how much, say, real GDP grew last year, the year before that, and so on until the beginning of the data series. Then, a weighted average of all those amounts of growth is calculated. Growth in the more recent years gets more weight. How much more? That depends. The amount of weight given to the more recent data can be varied by adjusting a coefficient, usually denoted by $\alpha$, in the exponential smoothing technique. If $\alpha = 1$, then only the growth of the most recent year is considered. The previous years are given weights of zero. Typically, $\alpha$ lies between zero and one. If $\alpha$ is set equal to, say, 0.1, then the most recent year gets a weight of 0.1. Each previous year is given less and less weight based on an exponential formula. Thus, the name "exponential smoothing."

The selection of an appropriate value for $\alpha$ used to be a major drawback of exponential smoothing. Rules have been developed to help choose this value. In general, the more erratic a data series, the closer to zero $\alpha$ should be set. These days, we need not be overly concerned with the appropriate value of the exponential smoothing constant, $\alpha$. Any good forecasting software package can be employed to try each value of $\alpha$ from zero to one in increments of 0.01. The value of $\alpha$ that affords the best forecasts (had it been used to forecast the recent past) is chosen. With good software, all of this is done in a short time at the touch of a button.[2]

The simple exponential smoothing technique described here has been extended to allow for all the trend variations mentioned in connection with trend extrapolation. Exponential smoothing can also incorporate seasonal variations into its predictions. The Holt-Winters technique is exponential smoothing that simultaneously allows for a trend variation and seasonality in the forecast.[3]

Although exponential smoothing is used fairly often in business settings, it performs poorly with economic data. Considering that exponentially smoothed predictions are merely a weighted average of the past changes in a data series, the technique will never foresee a turning point. During periods of prolonged, smooth growth, exponential smoothing will work well, but so will virtually any technique. Its use in business, however, is often warranted. Exponential smoothing is fast, easy to apply, and slightly more sophisticated than trend extrapolation. If a forecast is required for each of a thousand items in inventory, this technique stands ready. Moreover, if the forecaster has reason to believe the data series will take off or die down in the near future, these assumptions can be incorporated into the prediction.

## ARIMA Models

Autoregressive integrated moving-average (ARIMA) models, or ARIMA forecasting, are sometimes referred to as the Box-Jenkins approach after the authors of the seminal and authoritative work on the topic (Box and Jenkins, 1970). Indeed, this approach has become so dominant that the term "time-series" analysis often is used synonymously with ARIMA analysis. Like trend extrapolation and exponential smoothing, ARIMA models "look back" at past values of the series to be forecasted in order to determine if there are any patterns or consistencies to be exploited. The Box-Jenkins approach to forecasting is popular enough that we consider it in some detail.

### Autoregressive Models

Let us begin by looking at a simple autoregressive model, the "AR" portion of an ARIMA model. An autoregressive model stipulates that the current value of a data series is a linear function of its past values. Thus, current real GDP might depend on its own values in the previous three years:

$$RGDP_t = C + a1\ RGDP_{t-1} + a2\ RGDP_{t-2} + a3\ RGDP_{t-3} + e_t,$$

where $C$ is a constant term; $a1$, $a2$, and $a3$ are weights given to the three previous values of $RGDP$; and $e_t$ is an error term that will be discussed shortly. $C$, $a1$, $a2$, and $a3$ are called the parameters of the model. In order to use the autoregressive equation to make predictions, these parameter values must be determined. Several techniques are applicable for determining these values. At this point, it is best simply to note that a computer program will come up with appropriate parameter values after the data for *RGDP* have been supplied. More information concerning parameter determination is given below.

Ignoring the error term, $e_t$, for the moment, and assuming parameter values have been obtained, one simply plugs in the three past values for *RGDP* to come up with a forecast for current *RGDP*. Or one could plug in the current value of *RGDP* (into $RGDP_{t-1}$) and its two prior values to obtain a forecast for next period's *RGDP*. Astute readers may notice that autoregressive forecasts are very similar to exponentially smoothed forecasts. Both use weighted averages of past values to formulate predictions. In fact, it can be shown that exponential smoothing is just a specific case of autoregressive forecasting. With exponential smoothing, the weights are forced to be geometrically declining while autoregressive models are not restricted in this manner.

The error term in the autoregressive formulation denotes the fact that the relationship between *RGDP* and its past values is not exact. There is some randomness. The difference between what we would expect *RGDP* to be, based on its past values, and its actual value is $e_t$. It is hoped that these error terms (for there is one for each time period) are relatively small. Large error terms would indicate that the autoregressive model is not working well, or, in econometric jargon, does not have a good fit. A model that does not fit well will probably, but not necessarily, forecast poorly.

Perhaps a better fit can be achieved if more previous values of *RGDP* were included in the equation. Techniques have been developed to help determine the appropriate number of lagged values to include in an autoregressive model. Even if these are employed, trial and error are a typical part of the determination process. If more past values of *RGDP* improve the performance of the model, they are included.

Let us say that we have annual data for *RGDP* from 1929 to 1994 and that the values of the parameters for our autoregressive model were determined to be: $C = -1,635.75$; $a1 = 1.53$; $a2 = -0.79$; $a3 = 0.27$. We are then in a position to derive a "forecast" for 1994:

$$RGDP_{1994} = -1,635.75 + 1.53\, RGDP_{1993} - 0.79\, RGDP_{1992} + 0.27\, RGDP_{1991}.$$

Filling in the values for *RGDP* in 1993, 1992, and 1991, and doing the

Table 5.2

**Autoregressive Forecasts of Real GDP**

| Year | Actual *RGDP* | Autoregressive forecast | Error |
|------|---------------|-------------------------|-------|
| 1991 | 4,867.6 | | |
| 1992 | 4,979.3 | | |
| 1993 | 5,134.5 | | |
| 1994 | 5,344.0 | 5,276.3 | −67.7 |
| 1995 | | 5,401.3 | |
| 1996 | | 5,522.7 | |

*Source*: U.S. Department of Commerce and author's calculations.

arithmetic yields $RGDP_{1994}$ = \$5,276.3 billion. This is known as an "in-sample" forecast since it can be checked against the actual value of *RGDP* in 1994, which was \$5,344.0. The difference between actual *RGDP* and the forecast, \$5,276.3 − \$5,344.0 = −\$67.7, is the value of $e_t$, the error term for 1994 (see Table 5.2).

A prediction for *RGDP* in 1995 (\$5,401.3) is obtained in a similar fashion since we have data for *RGDP* in 1994, 1993, and 1992. Forecasts for 1996 and beyond can be made by employing a "bootstrap" procedure. To formulate a forecast for 1996, we need the three previous values for *RGDP*. We do not, however, have a value for *RGDP* in 1995 (assuming our data set only runs through 1994), unless we use our forecasted value of \$5,401.3. Thus, we obtain a forecast for 1996 (\$5,522.7). To get a prediction for 1997, we may use the two forecasted values of *RGDP* in 1996 and 1995 along with the actual value from 1994. This bootstrap procedure can be carried on ad infinitum, but the accuracy of the forecasts may degenerate as we use forecasts to obtain more forecasts. On the other hand, it is possible for the forecast errors of successive periods to cancel each other out. More typically, the forecast errors tend to accumulate.

### *Autoregressive Moving Average Models*

The fun is just beginning. We may add some moving-average terms (MA) to the autoregressive (AR) equation to obtain an autoregressive moving-average (ARMA) model. Moving-average terms are nothing more than the previous forecast errors. Remember that each time a forecast is made, there will be an error term, $e_t$. These errors may help to improve subsequent forecasts. For instance, if the ARMA model gave a large overestimate of *RGDP* last period, perhaps next period's forecast should be adjusted downward. In fact, it might pay to consider not only the previous forecast error, but errors going back several periods. There may be some sort of pattern in the previous forecast errors to be exploited in making the next forecast.

ARMA models create forecasts based on the past values of the data series and the past forecast errors. By including moving-average terms in the analysis, we are attempting to improve forecast accuracy by taking into account previous forecast errors:

$$RGDP_t = C + a1\ RGDP_{t-1} + a2\ RGDP_{t-2} + a3\ RGDP_{t-3} + b1\ e_{t-1} + b2\ e_{t-2} + d_t.$$

The moving-average terms are represented by $e_{t-1}$ and $e_{t-2}$. Each moving-average term has a parameter attached to it—$b1$ and $b2$. The values of the moving-average terms, as discussed, are the forecast errors generated by the equation in the past. For instance, if the ARMA equation underestimated *RGDP* by $25.2 in 1994, then this figure would be plugged in for $e_{t-1}$ when $t$ is 1995. The forecast error in 1993 would be the value substituted for $e_{t-2}$.

The values of the parameters attached to the moving-average terms need to be determined. The determination procedure will be described a bit later. For now, it is enough to understand that $b1$ and $b2$ represent weights attached to the prior forecast errors.

An ARMA model may have one or many moving-average terms. The example under consideration here has two: $e_{t-1}$ and $e_{t-2}$. The optimal number of moving-average terms to include in any given model is not always easily determined. There are some procedures that will help, but, as with the number of autoregressive terms, trial and error is necessary. If the forecast error from two periods ago improves the current forecast, include it in the model. In essence, one needs to figure out how far to look back. How many previous forecast errors should be considered?

Even with the inclusion of the moving-average terms, the ARMA model is still not perfectly accurate. It will have its own forecast errors—the $d_t$'s. It is hoped that these will be smaller than the forecast errors from the autoregressive model. If not, one might as well stick

Figure 5.1 **Real GDP, 1929–94**

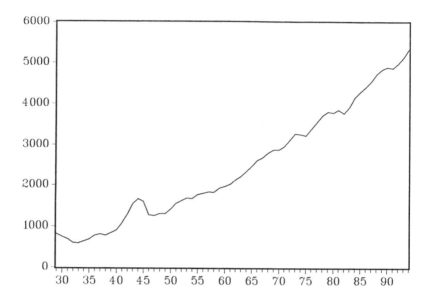

with the simple autoregressive model since the inclusion of the moving-average terms is not reducing the size of the forecast errors.

### *Integration*

Statistical theory indicates that ARMA models will not provide accurate forecasts unless the data series being forecasted has some special characteristics. Specifically, the data under consideration should have a constant mean, a constant variance, and a constant correlation among observations that are a given number of periods apart. A time series that exhibits these characteristics is said to be "weakly stationary." It will pay to develop an intuitive grasp of this concept because it sheds light on how ARMA models work.

Data series that exhibit trends, upward or downward, are not weakly stationary because they do not have a constant mean. Consider the *RGDP* data shown in Figure 5.1. The figure displays a pronounced upward trend. Thus, the average value of *RGDP* from 1929 to 1960 is $1,258.6, while its average from 1961 to 1994 is $3,608.2. Because of the upward trend, a later time period will always have a higher mean value than an earlier one. The average value of any data series with a trend is not constant.

Figure 5.2 **First Differences in Real GDP, 1930–94**

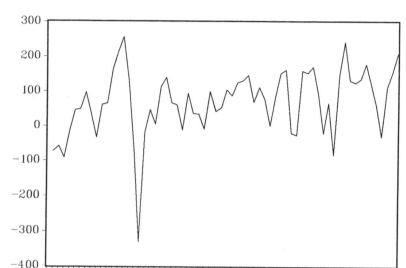

At this point the reader may be wondering how common ARMA models are in economic forecasting since these models perform poorly when applied to data series with trends. Most economic data exhibit trends. This, as it turns out, is not an impediment to the use of ARMA models in economic forecasting because it is a simple matter to detrend data. In practice, time series with trends are typically first-differenced to achieve a constant mean. First-differencing means taking the change in the time-series from one period to the next (see Figure 5.2).

The changes in *RGDP* have no pronounced trend and thus meet the first requirement for weak stationarity. If an ARMA model is applied to the differenced *RGDP* data, the forecasts will be for the change in *RGDP*, not the level of *RGDP*. But this is not a drawback, since a forecast for the level of *RGDP* can easily be obtained once a prediction for the change in *RGDP* is in hand.

Occasionally, the first-differences of a time series will continue to exhibit a trend. Then the differences of the differences, what is known as second-differences, may be taken. Indeed, a data series may be differenced any number of times until a constant mean is achieved. Economic data rarely require third-differences.

It is somewhat of a misnomer, but taking differences to attain

Figure 5.3 **A Time Series with Nonconstant Variance**

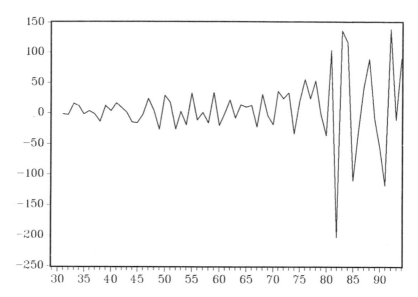

stationarity is known as "integration" in time-series forecasting. Thus, an autoregressive moving-average (ARMA) model becomes an autoregressive integrated moving-average (ARIMA) model when the data series to be forecasted is differenced.

The second requirement of weak stationarity is that the data display a constant variance. This implies that the figures should, on average, diverge from their mean value by the same amount in any given time period. The time series pictured in Figure 5.3 does not meet this requirement. The latter portion of the data tends to fluctuate more widely than earlier periods.[4]

If we look back at Figure 5.2, which depicts first-differenced *RGDP,* it is difficult to say whether or not that time series has a constant variance. Certainly, larger than normal deviations occurred in the 1940s. The variance of *RGDP* in the 1940s was almost three times higher than usual. On the other hand, this could be just an aberration. If it were not for the large variances in the 1940s, a rather constant variance would prevail throughout the entire sample period. Let us say that the constant-variance assumption is met by first-differenced *RGDP.*[5]

The third characteristic of weak stationarity is most important for the application of ARIMA models. It states that observations that are a given number of periods apart should have a constant covariance.

Let us say that, in a given data series, the value of every other observation is correlated to a certain extent. Then, according to the third condition for weak stationarity, the first and third observations, the second and fourth observations, and so on, must be correlated in the same way and to the same degree. ARIMA models attempt to exploit these relationships between observations. If the relationships are not stable, it will be impossible to exploit them effectively.

If it is known that every other observation of *RGDP* is related, then the ARIMA model should look back at least two periods. That is, the value of *RGDP* two periods ago should be used to predict *RGDP* this period. What is more, if this relationship is consistently strong, then we would want to place a lot of weight on it (by attaching a significantly large parameter to it). If the correlation is sometimes strong and sometimes weak, it is not clear how much emphasis should be placed on the observation two periods earlier. Things could be worse: no relationship at all may exist between current *RGDP* and *RGDP* two, or any number of periods ago. Although this situation is stationary (all the relationships are constant at zero correlation), there is nothing on which to base a prediction.

To summarize this section to this point, ARMA models are not applicable to time series that are not weakly stationary. Weakly stationary time series meet three requirements: they have a constant (1) mean, (2) variance, and (3) correlation between observations a given number of periods apart. Conditions (1) and (2) are easily verified by considering a plot of the data. If the data display a long-term trend or changing volatility, these conditions are violated. First- or higher-order differencing can usually correct such violations. Differencing the data is known as "integration" in time-series lingo and changes the ARMA model into an ARIMA model.

So far, nothing has been said about determining if the third condition of weak stationarity is met. And, in practice, the condition of constant correlation is simply assumed to hold true. ARIMA modelers carefully comb through the data to discern the relationship between observations spaced one, two, three, up to forty-eight periods apart in some cases. Yet, once it is established that observations, say, four periods apart are moderately correlated, no attempt is made to discern if that moderate correlation is constant throughout the entire data series. Perhaps earlier observations spaced four periods apart are strongly correlated, and later observations (also spaced four apart) are only weakly correlated, giving an overall appearance of moderate correlation. In such an instance, the third condition of weak stationarity is violated.

But how would one know if the observations spaced four periods apart were correlated or not? This is easy: Take all the pairs of observations so spaced in the data set and calculate a correlation coefficient. The correlation coefficient is a statistic that ranges between positive one and negative one and gives the degree to which two variables are linearly correlated. A reading of plus one means the observations are perfectly linked and move in the same direction. A reading of negative one also indicates a perfect relationship, except in this instance the observations move in the opposite direction. Finally, correlation coefficients around zero imply no relationship exists.

The implications of these correlations for forecasting should be made clear. If observations four periods apart have a correlation of +0.9, it would be advantageous to consider what happened three periods ago when making a prediction for the fourth period. Put another way, the ARIMA model should "look back" to that value as it generates a forecast.

### A Complete Example

Let us employ an ARIMA model to forecast *RGDP*. To do so, all we need is the past values of *RGDP*. The more past data available for the modeling procedure, the better. ARIMA forecasters prefer to use at least fifty observations covering an uninterrupted sample period of the immediate past. This is necessary to firmly establish the correlations between observations. Also, the favored procedure for estimating the parameters of an ARIMA model is more reliable the greater the number of past observations. The economic literature is sprinkled with examples of ARIMA models that are estimated with fewer than fifty observations, but these typically include a caution regarding the paucity of data.

Say we have sixty-two annual observations of *RGDP* from 1933 to 1994. The first task is to discern if these data are weakly stationary. As we saw in the previous section, they are not. However, the first-differences of *RGDP* are (arguably) weakly stationary. We shall work with these changes in *RGDP* and generate forecasts for them.

The next step is to determine how many autoregressive and how many moving-average terms to include in the model. There are several procedures that can help with this determination but trial and error are involved in any case.[6] If adding an extra autoregressive or moving-average term improves the forecast accuracy of the model, it should be included. It is possible to check forecast accuracy by having the model generate "forecasts" for previous years. For annual *RGDP*, the model we specified previously works about as well as any other:

$$RGDP_t = C + a1\ RGDP_{t-1} + a2\ RGDP_{t-2} +$$
$$a3\ RGDP_{t-3} + b1\ e_{t-1} + b2\ e_{t-2} + d_t.$$

There are three autoregressive terms and two moving-average terms in this model. Also, keep in mind that we are working with the differences in *RGDP*, not the levels. The common notation used to denote this specification is ARIMA(3,1,2); where the 3 indicates the number of autoregressive terms, 1 represents the number of times the data have been differenced, and 2 is for the two moving-average terms.

Before forecasts can be made, the values of the parameters ($C$, $a1$, $a2$, $a3$, $b1$, and $b2$) must be determined. Several techniques are available for this task. All are computationally cumbersome. Fortunately, readily available computer software handles the number crunching. The predominant technique for parameter determination in ARIMA models is known as the "maximum likelihood" procedure:

1.  Initial values for C, $a1$, $a2$, $a3$, $b1$, and $b2$ are selected. Usually the forecaster has no clue as to what the appropriate values might be, so they are all initially set equal to 0.5. In any case, the selection of initial values is arbitrary.

2.  The initial values are used to generate "forecasts" for the sample period. Since we have the actual *RGDP* data for the sample period, these forecasts can be checked for accuracy.

3.  The values of the parameters are revised in accordance with the maximum likelihood algorithm and the "forecast" errors in order to reduce the size of the errors.

4.  Return to step 2 with the revised parameter estimates.

5.  The procedure stops when the revisions made to the parameter values in step 3 are insignificant.

Thus, the maximum likelihood procedure selects parameter values that have resulted in the best forecast performance in the past. This, of course, is no guarantee that these values are optimal for forecasts that extend into the future.

For our *RGDP* example, with its sixty-two observations and ARIMA(3,1,2) specification, the maximum likelihood procedure results in the following parameter estimates:

$$C = 76.22;$$
$$a1 = 0.42;$$
$$a2 = 0.23;$$
$$a3 = -0.31;$$
$$b1 = 0.06;$$
$$b2 = -0.41;$$

The computer software employed for this task had to reiterate steps 2 through 4 of the procedure five times before the revisions in the parameter estimates did not change significantly. It took less than thirty seconds.

We now have all the information necessary to generate forecasts from the ARIMA(3,1,2) model. Past values of the differences in *RGDP* are plugged into the autoregressive portion of the equation. The forecast errors from the appropriate periods are plugged into the moving-average terms. Finally, predictions for the differences, or changes, in *RGDP* are obtained. Once the change in *RGDP* is predicted, it can be added to the previous level of *RGDP* to get a forecast of the level of *RGDP* (see Table 5.3).

The forecast error for 1994, 98.2, is larger than that of the purely autoregressive model. So, at least for that year, the addition of the two moving-average terms has not served to improve forecast accuracy. The forecast performance of ARIMA models is discussed in detail and compared with other forecasting techniques in chapter 8. At this point, it is sufficient to observe that ARIMA forecasts can compete quite well with other types of forecasts as far as accuracy is concerned.[7]

Every economic forecasting technique, however, encounters difficulty calling turning points, and ARIMA models are no exception. If we use our ARIMA(3,1,2) model to generate "forecasts" of *RGDP* from 1972 until 1994, it becomes apparent that the model is surprised by turns in the data (see Figure 5.4).

Table 5.3

**ARIMA Forecasts of Real GDP**

| Year | Actual *RGDP* | ARIMA forecast | Error |
|------|------|------|------|
| 1991 | 4,867.6 | | |
| 1992 | 4,979.3 | | |
| 1993 | 5,134.5 | | |
| 1994 | 5,344.0 | 5,245.8 | 98.2 |
| 1995 | | 5,323.5 | |
| 1996 | | 5,383.9 | |

*Source*: U.S. Department of Commerce and author's calculations.

The forecasts for *RGDP* appear to be a step behind actual *RGDP*. In 1973, when *RGDP* turns down with the recession, the ARIMA forecast continues to climb. This is because the ARIMA model looks back to make its prediction and sees no reason to turn down. Once the actual data begin to decline, the ARIMA model can detect this after the fact. The ARIMA forecasts then begin to fall, but too late.

ARIMA forecasts perform better during periods when there are no sharp turns in the data. Such a period occurred during the 1980s. Even here, there is a long stretch during which our ARIMA model consistently underpredicted *RGDP*.

### Trends: Stationary, Stochastic, and Chaotic

ARIMA models attempt to exploit patterns and trends in the past values of a data series to make forecasts of future values. This approach will be fruitless if there are no patterns and trends to exploit. Recent developments in trend analysis with economic data suggest that there may be patterns, but these patterns are continually changing in an unpredictable way. This section considers these developments and their implications for time-series forecasting.

#### *Time-Series Decomposition*

It is an old idea that a time series can be decomposed, taken apart, into several components. The figure for GDP in any given quarter can be thought of as consisting of these elements: (1) a long-term trend, (2) a

Figure 5.4 **Actual Real GDP and Forecasted Real GDP, 1972–94**

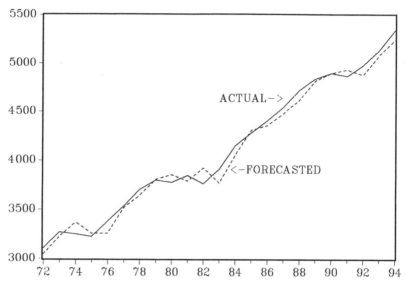

short-term trend, (3) an irregular component, and, perhaps, (4) a seasonal component. Techniques for decomposing a time series into its essential elements have been developed. Indeed, seasonal adjustment of data is nothing more than purging a time series of its seasonal component.

Conventional wisdom in economics holds that the long-term trends in macroeconomic time series are, more or less, stable. The long-term trend in GDP, for example, may rise or fall in accordance with such things as population and productivity, but it is well behaved. That is, changes in the long-term trend in GDP can be explained by predetermined factors and can be predicted with equations. The short-term trend, or cyclical component, is also thought to be explainable. The economic factors that result in business cycles explain why GDP is deviating from its long-term trend. Only the irregular component—random deviations from the long- and short-term trends—is unexplainable.

The best a forecaster can do is to pick up on the long-term and cyclical trends. The random component of a time series, by definition, can never be explained, let alone predicted. Since forecast errors are the difference between the actual and the predicted value of a time series, they should be random. If a forecaster consistently over- or underpredicted, or revealed any systematic sort of error process, then those predictions could be improved by taking the error pattern into consideration and adjusting the forecasts accordingly. Since the forecast errors are not random, as is the irregular component of a time series, then the forecast is not doing a good job of predicting the components that are foreseeable: the long- and short-term trends. Forecasting, thus, becomes an exercise in mimicking the deterministic portion of a data series.

Following this methodology, ARIMA models attempt to capture the deterministic, or explainable, portion of a given data series. Once this has been accomplished, the ARIMA equation can be used to forecast future values of the series. The difference between the realized values and the forecasts should be random, reflecting the irregular component of the time series that the ARIMA model could not hope to capture. Forecasts that result in nonrandom errors are said to be biased.

### Stationary and Stochastic Trends

The idea that macroeconomic time series are comprised of deterministic long- and short-term trends plus a random component was brought into question with the work of Nelson and Plosser.[8] These authors use the term "trend-stationary" to describe the traditional view of macroeconomic time series: data with a deterministic long-term trend, a deterministic short-term trend that oscillates around the long-term trend, and a bit of real-world randomness thrown in. Nelson and Plosser's results suggest that most macroeconomic time series are not trend-stationary, but instead, "difference-stationary." "Difference-stationary" refers to time series that essentially have no long-term trend because the forces that shape this trend are unpredictable and vary widely even over short periods. This situation is sometimes indicated by stating that the time series has a stochastic, as opposed to stationary, long-term trend.

Nelson and Plosser's paper was seminal, spawning myriad investigations into the nature of macroeconomic time series.[9] A variety of initial assumptions and statistical techniques have been brought to bear on the topic, with inconsistent results. A statistician would say that the test results concerning trend stationarity are not robust—meaning different test procedures give different results. Much of the statistical work involves a search for "unit autoregressive roots" in macroeconomic time series.[10] If the time series contains a unit root, it is said to be "integrated" and therefore not trend-stationary.

The concept of trend stationarity is important in several respects. For the application of ARIMA techniques, the data must be at least weakly stationary. If a data series is not stationary, it would have to be differenced before an ARIMA model could be applied. Moreover, if macroeconomic data are not trend-stationary, this contradicts standard business-cycle analysis, which presupposes that business cycles revolve around stationary long-term trends. Stochastic trends in macroeconomic data support the essence of "real" business-cycle theory: factors affecting the long-term trend change even in the short run, resulting in business cycles and obliterating the stability of the long-term trend. Thus, the idea of trend stationarity is important for preserving the traditional view of cyclical fluctuations. Moreover, macroeconomic forecasting becomes more precarious if the long-term trend is subject to stochastic changes in the short run.[11]

### Chaos

A recent development in mathematics has provided yet another perspective from which to consider macroeconomic data. The development is referred to as "chaos," or, more formally, "nonlinear dynamics."[12] A data series is said to be chaotic when it appears to be a random string of numbers but is actually determined by a nonlinear function (with, perhaps, a bit of randomness thrown in). Consider the following string of integers:

$$3, 9, 81, 6, 561, \ldots$$

A bit of scrutiny reveals the determining function to be:

$$X_t = X_{t-1}^2.$$

That is, each entry is the square of its predecessor. Although the entries are determined by a nonlinear function, the string is not chaotic since it does not appear to be random even to the naked eye. In a truly random set of numbers, each entry would not be larger than its predecessor.

Tests have been developed to determine if a string of numbers is random. The following string of numbers (only the first five of forty are shown) passed two such tests, indicating that they are random numbers between zero and one:[13]

$$0.0000, 0.0263, 0.1511, 0.4121, 0.3222, \ldots$$

Yet, the numbers are not truly random, but are generated by the following nonlinear formulation:

$$X_t = Z_t / 4, 294, 967, 299,$$

where $Z_t = (16,807 \cdot Z_{t-1})$ MOD $4, 294, 967, 299$. (The notation $A$ MOD $B$ means the remainder when $A$ is divided by $B$. Also, the initial value of $Z_{t-1}$ must be given. In this case it was 0.4.)

This formulation is often used to generate "random" numbers in computer programs. But if the formulation is known, one could perfectly forecast the entire string of numbers given the first. The data series appears to be random, but it is not. It is determined by a nonlinear function and is, therefore, classified as chaotic. Thus, chaotic series of numbers appear random but have an underlying order. Finding the underlying order is, in most cases, nearly impossible. There are an infinite number of possible nonlinear formulations and, in the real world, a dose of pure randomness may be added to the nonlinear equation.

Are business and economic data characterized by chaos? The final results are not in yet, but there is some evidence to consider. Chaotic systems are extremely sensitive to initial conditions. This means that if one number in a chaotic string is slightly altered, all the subsequent numbers will be markedly different. It is not clear that economic data are similarly sensitive. If GDP were a mere billion dollars different than it was three years ago, would it be a vastly different figure today? Another piece of evidence involves what chaos analysts call bifurcations: sudden and major breaks in the data. Certainly, a case could be made for these in economics and business (especially the financial markets).

William Brock of the University of Wisconsin has provided the most damning evidence against chaos in macroeconomic time series.[14] He finds that although there are indications of nonlinearities in macroeconomic time series, evidence of low-level (relatively uncomplicated) chaos is weak. Stock market data also show no evidence of chaos.[15]

These conclusions concerning the absence of chaos in business and economic data are preliminary and tentative. The power of the tests used to reach these conclusions is uncertain. Chaos is such a new area of research that the techniques for testing for its presence are not well established.

Perhaps more important, once a time series is determined to be chaotic, there is no method or strategy for discovering the underlying nonlinear mechanism that drives it. There is an unlimited number of nonlinear mechanisms. Thus, chaos theory is years away from delivering any payoffs in the field of economic forecasting and it is possible that there never will be any payoff.

If a particular economic or business time series is determined to be chaotic and its underlying order can be discovered, economic forecasting would be greatly facilitated. Still, forecasting would not be an exact science. Remember, chaotic series are sensitive to initial conditions. So, if there is a measurement error or some other discrepancy in the data for this period, forecasted future values could be far off. And, in practice, it is improbable that economic data are purely chaotic. If they are chaotic, that chaos is probably augmented with random movements in the data—what statisticians call "white noise." These facts are not enough to discourage research in the field of chaos. The potential payoffs are large enough to warrant further investigation.

**Summary**

This chapter has presented the time-series techniques used in business and economic forecasting. Trend extrapolation has been shown to be a rather naive forecasting procedure for macroeconomic variables such as real GDP. Because of the business cycle, economic variables are usually not growing at their average rate. Nevertheless, trend extrapolation may work better in the long run, when the ups and downs of the business cycle have a tendency to wash each other out.

Because exponential smoothing is just a fancy trend extrapolation procedure, it is given short shrift in this chapter and by economic forecasters. Moreover, it can be shown that exponential smoothing is a special case of the more general ARIMA forecasting procedure.

Autoregressive integrated moving-average models (ARIMA) are computationally cumbersome, but based on a simple strategy: exploit any patterns exhibited in the past values of a data series to predict future values of that series. The computational drudgery is handled by computers, which makes ARIMA forecasting rather attractive. The forecaster must supply an uninterrupted string of about fifty periods or more of the variable to be forecasted. Then, the number of autoregressive and moving-average terms must be selected. There are procedures to help with this selection, but in practice, a good deal of trial and error is involved. If two autoregressive terms and two moving-average terms are providing reasonable forecasts, then try adding another autoregressive term and/or another moving-average term to the model. Does this improve the forecasts over a sample period that can be checked? Then go with the improved version of the ARIMA model.

This chapter concluded by mentioning some recent developments in the analysis of macroeconomic time series. If a time series is not trend-stationary, then the forecasting techniques presented in this chapter are not applicable. If trend extrapolation or an ARIMA model is used on data that have a stochastic trend, then accurate forecasts would not be expected. The question of whether or not most macroeconomic data are characterized by stochastic trends has not yet been answered definitively. Another possibility is that the macroeconomy is characterized by chaos. In this event, forecasting would be a snap if only we could uncover the nonlinear dynamics that drive the economy. At this time, the chaos approach to forecasting is in an embryonic stage.

### Notes

1. Another technique for resolving this difficulty is "discounted least squares." We do not pursue this procedure here since it yields results similar to exponential smoothing. See Newbold and Bos (1990, pp. 190–91) for more information on discounted least squares.

2. My students ask why we spend so much time learning exponential smoothing when a computer can handle the procedure so easily. My response: "What do you tell the boss when she asks why your forecast failed so miserably last year?"

3. See Newbold and Bos (1990, chapter 6) for more details on all of these smoothing techniques.

4. The time series that displays nonconstant variance is actually nominal GDP (GDP not adjusted for inflation) after taking second-differences.

5. In this particular case, taking second-differences does not improve the situation.

6. See Newbold and Bos (1990, chapter 7) for details on how autocorrelations, partial autocorrelations, the Akaike Information Criterion, and the Schwartz Bayesian Criterion are used to help determine the number of autoregressive and moving-average terms to include in any particular ARIMA model.

7. In two articles, Charles Nelson (1972, 1984) demonstrates that ARIMA forecasts are approximately as accurate as econometric forecasts.

8. See Nelson and Plosser (1982). Also, see Hall (1978) for the first salvo against classical time-series decomposition for macroeconomic data.

9. See DeJong and Whiteman (1991) for a recent example.

10. See Sims and Uhlig (1991) and Christiano, Eichenbaum, and Stock (1990) for the details of the search for unit roots.

11. See Balke (1991), who claims that forecasting inflation is extremely difficult because price movements are characterized by a stochastic trend.

12. See Gleick (1987) for an accessible and intriguing account of the development of this field of mathematics. Also, see Baumol and Benhabib (1989) for a survey of the application of chaos analysis in economics.

13. Specifically, the string of numbers passed the *Kolmogorov–Smirnov* test and the *runs* test. See Banks and Carson (1984, pp. 267–76) for the details of these tests.

14. See Brock (1986) and Brock and Sayers (1988).

15. See Hsieh (1991).

## References

Balke, Nathan S. 1991. "Modeling Trends in Macroeconomic Time Series." *Economic Review—Federal Reserve Bank of Dallas* (May): 19–33.

Banks, Jerry, and Carson, John S. 1984. *Discrete-Event System Simulation.* Englewood Cliffs, NJ: Prentice-Hall.

Baumol, William J., and Benhabib, Jess. 1989. "Chaos: Significance, Mechanism, and Economic Applications." *Journal of Economic Perspectives* (Winter): 77–105.

Box, G.E.P., and Jenkins, G.M. 1970. *Time Series Analysis: Forecasting and Control.* San Francisco: Holden Day.

Brock, William A. 1986. "Distinguishing Random and Deterministic Systems: Abridged Version." *Journal of Economic Theory,* 40: 168–95.

Brock, W.A., and Sayers, C.L. 1988. "Is the Business Cycle Characterized by Deterministic Chaos?" *Journal of Monetary Economics* (July): 71–90.

Christiano, L.; Eichenbaum, M.; and Stock, J. 1990. "Unit Roots in Real GNP: Do We Know, and Do We Care?; Comment." *Carnegie-Rochester Conference Series on Public Policy,* 32 (Spring): 7–82.

DeJong, David N., and Whiteman, Charles H. 1991. "Reconsidering 'Trends and Random Walks in Macroeconomic Time Series'." *Journal of Monetary Economics,* 28: 221–54.

Gleick, James. 1987. *Chaos: Making a New Science.* New York: Viking.

Hall, Robert E. 1978. "Stochastic Implications of the Life Cycle–Permanent Income Hypothesis: Theory and Evidence." *Journal of Political Economy,* 86: 971–88.

Hsieh, David A. 1991. "Chaos and Nonlinear Dynamics: Application to Financial Markets." *Journal of Finance* (December): 1839–77.

Nelson, Charles R. 1972. "The Prediction Performance of the FRB–MIT–Penn Model of the U.S. Economy." *American Economic Review* (December): 902–17.

————. 1984. "A Benchmark for the Accuracy of Econometric Forecasts of GNP." *Business Economics* (April): 52–58.

Nelson, Charles R., and Plosser, Charles I. 1982. "Trends and Random Walks in Macroeconomic Time Series." *Journal of Monetary Economics,* 10: 139–62.

Newbold, Paul, and Bos, Theodore. 1990. *Introductory Business Forecasting.* Cincinnati, OH: South-Western.

Sims, Christopher A., and Uhlig, Harald. 1991. "Understanding Unit Rooters: A Helicopter Tour." *Econometrica* (November): 1591–99.

# 6

# Forecasting with Econometric Models

> The deductive science of economy must be verified and rendered use-
> ful by the purely inductive science of statistics.
>
> —S. Jevons, 1871

Mathematical models, with hundreds of equations, have become the predominant approach to making economic forecasts. The statistical theory behind this technique and the economic theory embedded in the individual equations is formidable. Nevertheless, an intuitive understanding of the essential ideas of economic modeling can be obtained rather easily. That is the purpose of this chapter.

## Introduction

The term "model" may seem peculiar to some readers, but it is appropriate. The hundreds of equations that comprise a large-scale econometric model are an attempt to simulate the workings of the economy. Consider this analogy: Large-scale econometric models are like the small-scale replicas an inventor might use to test a new machine. The replica spins and whirs to reveal how the individual parts will operate as a whole once the machine is set in motion. Similarly, the numerical values in the equations of the econometric model will rise and fall, once the model is set in motion, simulating the reactions of the real-world economy. The model can be used to forecast the behavior of the macroeconomy in response to a variety of stimuli.

As we shall see, econometric modeling is a precarious task with unavoidable pitfalls and discouraging drawbacks. Yet, these models dominate the field of economic forecasting with good reason. One of these reasons is that technical advances, not only in mathematics and statistics but also in computation (i.e., the computer), have made macro modeling a more feasible and attractive endeavor. Another, perhaps more substantial, explanation for the rise of econometric modeling is the reliance of the models on economic theory. As we have seen, time-series models and, to a large extent, indicator forecasting have not utilized economic theory. These latter techniques therefore have nothing to offer in the way of economic explanation for the forecasts they produce.

The equations in macroeconomic models are mathematical statements of economic theory. When theory provides detailed and precise explanations of economic behavior, the econometrician stands on firm ground. Where economic theory is ambiguous, the econometrician is uncertain about mathematical formulation. Putting aside one's opinion about the precision of economic theory, econometric models can provide insight as to how the economy functions. One is able to discern the source of trouble, where a relationship is breaking down, or why a particular variable is increasing or decreasing.

With these insights, macro modelers are able to adjust their models to conform more closely with reality. Every econometric forecast is adjusted in light of current events and changes in the economic landscape. Poor forecasts imply that some part or parts of the model are not simulating reality appropriately. The faulty equations are, in most cases, obvious and the subject of adjustment.

Changing economic relationships and model adjustments can be troublesome. But the fact that macro models are open to adjustment and often themselves suggest where changes should be made is another explanation for the dominance of this type of forecasting.

Consider this example: Wharton Econometric Forecasting Associates (WEFA) has about 800 equations in its econometric model of the U.S. economy. The current model is referred to as the Mark 9, an indication of the number of major structural adjustments it has undergone. WEFA provides an array of forecasting services and, like its competitors, relies on analysis of current events and other forecasting techniques (economic indicators and time-series models) to adjust the base forecasts obtained from the Mark 9.

WEFA's strongest competition comes from Data Resources Incor-
porated/McGraw-Hill (DRI), another private firm. Both WEFA and
DRI, however, have their roots in academia. WEFA was founded in
1963 by professor and Nobel Prize laureate Lawrence Klein and was
initially housed at the Wharton School of the University of Pennsylvania. DRI was founded in 1969 by the late Otto Eckstein, a professor of
economics at Harvard. WEFA and DRI are the best-known
macroeconometric models in the private sector, but there are many
others. Many brokerage houses have developed their own models, such
as that of Merrill Lynch Economics, Incorporated. And then there are
the models that are still housed in academia but bring profit and pres-
tige to their institutions. The major players in this arena are the Economic Forecasting Center at Georgia State University, the Research
Seminar in Quantitative Economics at the University of Michigan, and
the Business Forecasting Project at the University of California, Los
Angeles.

To understand how econometric models are used to generate forecasts, it is best to start with a small, simple model. Before we can
undertake this, one must understand regression analysis—how a single
equation can capture economic relationships.

**Regression Analysis**

Econometrics literally means economic measurement. One of its leading practitioners, Henri Theil, defines econometrics as "the empirical
determination of economic laws."[1] Less concisely, econometrics ap-
plies statistical techniques to the relevant data in order to discern the
relationships among economic variables. Once these relationships are
spelled out, they may be used to make forecasts. For instance, suppose
we know that housing starts increase by about 81,000 units per year for
each 1 percent drop in the interest rate. Then, one would predict a
121,500-unit increase in housing starts for a year in which interest
rates were expected to fall by 1.5 percent ($121,500 = 81,000 \times 1.5$).
Simple, but how does one determine that housing starts increase
81,000 units per year for each percentage-point decline in the interest
rate? The answer is regression analysis.

Regression analysis is a statistical technique for discerning the relationship between two or more variables. Let us begin with the simple
case of two variables. Table 6.1 shows the data for two variables, $Y$

Table 6.1

**Annual Observations on Y and X**

| Year | Y | X |
|------|------|-------|
| 1948 | 79 | 0.33 |
| 1949 | 86 | 0.15 |
| 1950 | 478 | 0.07 |
| 1951 | −488 | 0.49 |
| 1952 | 26 | 0.44 |
| 1953 | −44 | 0.17 |
| 1954 | 130 | −0.12 |
| 1955 | 95 | 0.11 |
| 1956 | −302 | 0.61 |
| 1957 | −150 | 0.43 |
| 1958 | 139 | −0.37 |
| 1959 | 203 | 0.65 |
| 1960 | −265 | 0.34 |
| 1961 | 61 | −0.32 |
| 1962 | 150 | 0.00 |
| 1963 | 140 | 0.00 |
| 1964 | −74 | 0.00 |
| 1965 | −56 | 0.04 |
| 1966 | −308 | 1.09 |
| 1967 | 127 | 0.00 |
| 1968 | 216 | 0.65 |
| 1969 | −41 | 1.67 |
| 1970 | −33 | −0.04 |
| 1971 | 618 | −2.21 |
| 1972 | 305 | −0.45 |
| 1973 | −312 | 2.77 |
| 1974 | −707 | 2.78 |
| 1975 | −178 | −2.94 |
| 1976 | 378 | −1.02 |
| 1977 | 449 | −0.02 |
| 1978 | 33 | 2.24 |
| 1979 | −275 | 3.61 |
| 1980 | −453 | 2.60 |
| 1981 | −208 | 3.60 |
| 1982 | −22 | −4.01 |
| 1983 | 641 | −4.07 |
| 1984 | 47 | 1.25 |
| 1985 | −8 | −2.11 |
| 1986 | 63 | −1.60 |
| 1987 | −185 | −0.13 |
| 1988 | −132 | 1.12 |
| 1989 | −112 | 1.55 |
| 1990 | −183 | −0.86 |
| 1991 | −179 | −1.55 |
| 1992 | 186 | −2.21 |
| 1993 | 88 | −0.25 |
| 1994 | 169 | 1.14 |

Figure 6.1 **Observations on X and Y**

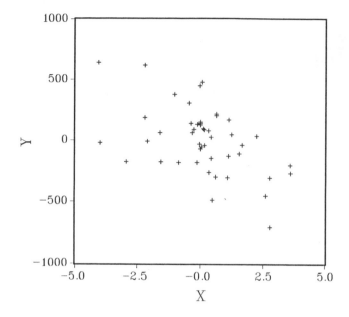

and $X$. It is not easy to determine the relationship between $Y$ and $X$ with the naked eye, but a bit of scrutiny reveals that $Y$ typically moves in the opposite direction from $X$. Beginning with the first value of $Y$, 79, we see that it increases to 86 in 1949. Meanwhile, $X$ has decreased to 0.15 from 0.33. From 1950 to 1951, $Y$ decreases while $X$ increases. Although $X$ and $Y$ do not always change conversely (as in 1952–53, when both declined), they do in general. It is said that $X$ and $Y$ have an "inverse," or "negative," relationship.

This relationship is made more clear through a graph of the data, such as Figure 6.1. The values of $Y$ are plotted along the vertical axis and the values of $X$ along the horizontal axis. Each dot represents a year, or an "observation"—a $Y$ value and the corresponding $X$ value. This sort of diagram is called a "scattergram" in econometrics. The observations in Figure 6.1 are splayed in a downward fashion from left to right. This indicates an inverse relationship. When $X$ is low (near the origin), $Y$ is typically high (away from the origin) and vice versa.

If a scattergram shows the observations to be sloping upward from left to right, then a "direct," or "positive," relationship between the two variables is indicated. That is to say, $X$ and $Y$ generally move in the same direction. If no pattern at all is suggested by the scattergram, then $X$ and $Y$ may not be related.

Regression analysis is nothing more than fitting a line between the observations on a scattergram. There are several techniques available for accomplishing this task. Perhaps the simplest method would be to "eyeball" a line between the dots—just place the line where it appears appropriate. In the case depicted in Figure 6.1, the line would undoubtedly slope downward from left to right. We could then read off where this line intersected the vertical axis and we could calculate the slope of the line. That is, we could write a formula, based on the line, that describes the relationship between $X$ and $Y$ in slope intercept form:

$$Y = b1 + b2(X),$$

where $b1$ is the value of the vertical intercept and $b2$ is the value of the slope of the line.

There are several points to make about this formula. First, we know the numbers to plug in for $b1$ and $b2$ because they are merely the intercept and slope of the line we eyeballed into the scattergram. Second, it matters which variable appears on the left of the equality sign. The variable in this position, $Y$ in this case, is referred to as the "dependent" variable; its value depends on the value of $X$, the "independent" variable. Placing $Y$ to the left of the equality sign stipulates that it feels the effect, while $X$ is the cause of that effect.

We must now return to techniques for fitting lines between dots because the eyeball technique is not going to suffice in many instances. In a case where the splay of dots is not so obviously sloped, different eyes may see drastically different lines. A more objective technique is required. The most popular method for fitting a line on a scattergram is known as ordinary least squares. This technique places the line so that the sum of the squared distances from the dots to the line is minimized. Such a line, for the data on $Y$ and $X$ with which we are working, is shown in Figure 6.2.

Why minimize the *squared* distances? If the distances were not squared, the positive deviations and the negative deviations would cancel each other out. In fact, many different lines can be placed through the observations to yield a sum of the deviations equal to zero. Taking absolute values of the deviations before summing would solve this

Figure 6.2 **Observations on *X* and *Y* with Regression Line**

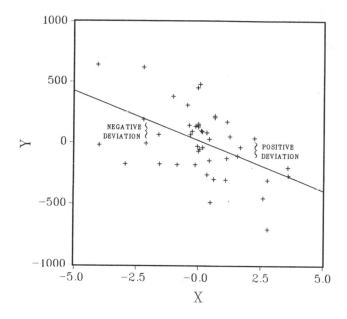

problem, but so does squaring. And minimizing the squared deviations results in a line with desirable statistical properties. Specifically, a line fit with the ordinary least squares technique is BLU—best, linear, and unbiased. The terms "best," "linear," and "unbiased" have statistical definitions apart from their use in everyday English. This is not the place to go into these definitions, or the finer details of regression analysis.[2] The concepts are raised to give the impression—for it is true—that a highly qualified line is fitted between the observations when the technique employed for the purpose minimizes the sum of the deviations squared.

Using ordinary least squares to establish a slope intercept relationship between variables is regression analysis. The term "regression analysis" is sometimes used more broadly to mean not only ordinary least squares but also interpretation of the results of the ordinary least squares technique. Let us take an example to demonstrate regression analysis.

The data on *Y* and *X* in Table 6.1 and depicted in Figures 6.1 and 6.2 are actually annual data on housing starts (*Y*) and the prime rate of interest (*X*) in the United States. The data are in first-difference form.

That is, the 79 in 1948 for housing starts means there were 79 (thousand) more housing starts in 1948 than in 1947. The 0.33 for the interest rate indicates that the prime rate rose 0.33 percent in 1948 from its level in 1947. Theoretically, the change in housing starts is affected by the change in the interest rate. The change in housing starts is therefore the dependent variable and the change in the prime rate is the independent variable:

$$STARTS = b1 + b2\ RATE.$$

Ordinary least squares will be used to find the values of $b1$ and $b2$. Indeed, the ordinary least squares line has already been drawn through the observations in Figure 6.2. We could read off the vertical intercept of that line and fill that number in for $b1$. We also could take the slope of that line and that would be the value of $b2$. In practice, $b1$ and $b2$ are calculated with formulas that have been derived to give the values of $b1$ and $b2$ that minimize the sum of the squared deviations.[3]

If the theory that rising interest rates result in declining housing starts is correct, then $b2$ will turn out to be a negative number. This is what Theil meant when he defined econometrics as the empirical determination of economic laws. Having obtained the data, we are determining whether interest rates have the hypothesized effect on housing starts. Given Figure 6.2, it would be impossible for $b2$, which represents the slope of the relationship, to be anything but negative. And, indeed, ordinary least squares results in values of 18.8 for $b1$ and $-81.7$ for $b2$.

These results could be used to make conditional forecasts. If interest rates fall by 1 percent, housing starts are expected to increase 62.9 (thousand) units: $\{62.9 = 18.8 - 81.7(-1)\}$. The problem here, as with any conditional forecast, is that a forecast of the change in interest rates is required to obtain a forecast of the change in housing starts.

Even if one nails the interest rate forecast, the resulting prediction for housing starts may be in error. The relationship between interest rates and housing starts is not exact and the regression results give the average relationship between the two variables over the years. This gives rise to a serious problem associated with regression analysis: The relationship between the two variables may have changed over the years. The regression gives the average relationship, which is not the same as the current relationship under these circumstances. Forecasts based upon the regression giving the average relationship will be biased. Fortunately, statistical tests have been developed to determine if the relationship has been restructured over time.[4]

The problem posed by conditional forecasts—that a forecast of the independent variable is required to obtain the forecast of the dependent variable—sometimes can be circumvented. In some cases, it turns out that the current value of the dependent variable (housing starts) depends on the *previous* value of the independent variable (interest rates):

$$STARTS_t = b1 + b2\ RATE_{t-1}.$$

The subscripts, $t$ and $t-1$, denote the lagged nature of this relationship. Housing starts this year ($t$) depend on interest rates last year ($t-1$). There is a theoretical explanation for the lag: Decisions on whether or not to begin new construction on housing depend on interest rates. When interest rates turn favorable, it takes some time to obtain a loan and a contractor and actually start the building.

This brings up the issue of the frequency of the data used in the regression. In our example, the data are annual. But we should be using quarterly data if interest rates this quarter affect the number of housing starts the next quarter. The appropriate frequency (annual, quarterly, monthly, weekly, daily, or hourly) depends on the nature of the relationship between the variables. It is important to consider the time frame involved.

For instance, a regression that explains the price of a corporation's stock with the profits of that firm ($STOCKPRICE = b1 + b2\ PROFITS$) should most likely use quarterly data since the profits of firms are generally reported on a quarterly basis. The point is not that quarterly data on profits will be available, but that decisions to buy or sell will be made on a quarterly basis. Investors focus on a firm's profit report each quarter and this motivates buying and selling, which, in turn, affects the price of the firm's equity. One could argue that in today's stock market, where analysts track the performance of large corporations, profit pictures are actually made available weekly or daily. If this is true and investors buy and sell on the basis of these estimates, then the time frame for the relationship between profits and equity prices is weekly or daily and data of this frequency should be used in the regression analysis.

Regardless of the frequency of the data used, if the regression embodies a lagged relationship, then unconditional forecasts can be made. Again, using the annual data on changes in housing starts and changes in the interest rate, the following regression was estimated:

$$STARTS_t = b1 + b2\ RATE_{t-1}.$$

In this case, ordinary least squares gives $b1 = 12.4$ and $b2 = -87.2$. Thus, if interest rates rise 1.25 percent this year, we would expect housing starts to decline 96.6 (thousand) units next year: $\{-96.6 = 12.4 - 87.2 (1.25)\}$.

There are several further points to consider before we close this section on regression analysis. Before we proceed, it should be made clear that there are entire textbooks devoted to regression analysis, while the goal here is to give the reader an intuitive grasp of the subject so that applications in economic forecasting can be understood. With this in mind, we broach the topic of multiple regression.

A regression equation is not limited to only one independent variable. In fact, forecasts based on regressions that do not include *all* the pertinent explanatory variables on the right-hand side of the equation will be biased. This is undoubtedly the case with our simple example concerning housing starts. There are other variables, aside from interest rates, that have a bearing on housing starts. The important ones, such as the level of income in the economy, should be included:

$$STARTS_t = b1 + b2\ RATE_t + b3\ INC_t.$$

One or both of the independent variables may have a lagged relationship with housing starts. The way the regression above is specified, the relationships are not lagged, but contemporaneous.

Adding another independent variable complicates the calculation of $b1$, $b2$, and now $b3$. However, since calculations are the computer's job, that is of no concern (except to the programmer). Conceptually, one is no longer fitting a line between dots, but rather, fitting a plane between dots in three dimensions (see Figure 6.3). The plane is fitted so that the squared distances from the observations to the plane are minimized. Thus, the ordinary least squares technique is applied in this case to give:

Figure 6.3 **Fitting a Plane**

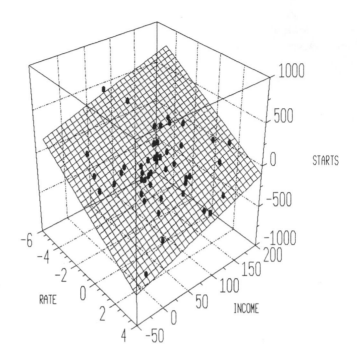

$$b1 = -136.6; \; b2 = -97.5; \; b3 = 2.1,$$

or

$$STARTS = -136.6 - 97.5 \; (RATE) + 2.1 \; (INC).$$

Remember that the actual data used for this regression are in first-differenced form. That is, we used data on the *change* in housing starts, the interest rate, and income, not their levels. With that in mind, we now conclude that a 1 percent rise in the interest rate, coupled with no change in income, is expected to lower housing starts by 234.1 (thousand) units over last year's figure (−234.1 = −136.6 − [97.5] 1). If income, on the other hand, did not remain unchanged, but increased by $1 (billion), then housing starts would only be expected to decline by 232.0 (thousand) units when interest rates rose by 1 percent:

$$-232.0 = -136.6 - (97.5) \, 1 + (2.1) \, 1.$$

Thus, this regression could be used to make conditional forecasts: If interest rates were to rise by 1.5 percent and income were to increase by $275 (billion), then housing starts would be expected to rise by 295.64 (thousand) over last year's level:

$$294.65 = -136.6 - (97.5)\ 1.5 + (2.1)\ 275.$$

If lagged relationships were used to develop the regression, unconditional forecasts could be made as we demonstrated in the case with only one independent variable.

A regression analysis may include any number of independent variables.[5] Techniques have been developed to determine if a particular independent variable belongs in a regression or not. Despite these, the best guide for determining what variables should be included is economic theory. If the variable theoretically has an important impact on the dependent variable, it should be included.

## Econometric Models

The housing starts regressions with which we have been working are sometimes referred to as econometric models. They resemble working replicas of the actual market for new housing. An analyst could change the interest rate or income in the model and observe the ensuing change in housing starts. In order to make forecasts about the entire economy, however, more than one equation is required, since housing starts are just one segment of the macroeconomy. And the segments are interrelated. For instance, housing starts are a determinant of employment in the construction industry. To forecast construction employment with a regression, the number of housing starts is required, this time as an independent variable:

$$CONEMPLOY = b1 + b2\ STARTS + b3\ CONWAGE.$$

In the regression above, employment in the construction industry (*CONEMPLOY*) depends on housing starts (*STARTS*) and the wage rate in construction (*CONWAGE*). Thus, an equation is required for each segment of the economy. These systems of interrelated regression equations are known as econometric models.

Jan Tinbergen was the first econometrician to build systems of equations reflecting the structure of an entire economy.6 His 1939 work was commissioned by the League of Nations. The model Tinbergen built was used to examine the business-cycle theories documented by Haberler (1937). Prominent economists of the time, including Keynes (1939) and Friedman (1940), criticized the effort. Their criticisms centered on the inability of the data and the statistical techniques to distinguish between the effects of the multifarious economic forces that can cause economic fluctuations.

Although the focus has shifted somewhat, econometric models today still serve as a lightning rod for debate. The modern criticism is that the models cannot hope to capture the complex and ever-changing relationships throughout the economy.7 Everything depends on everything and it is nigh impossible to disentangle the effects for forecasting purposes. And even if things could be sorted out, the relationships will soon change, thus scuttling any attempt at longer-term forecasting.

As noted, the first econometric models in the late 1930s and 1940s were built to investigate the causes of business cycles. Later models were built to study policies that would ameliorate economic fluctuations. But the forecasting potential of these systems of equations was always apparent.

A major schism developed between econometric modelers and other researchers of the business cycle in the 1940s. In order to develop their equations, the econometricians relied heavily on economic theory. Each equation embodied a piece of the theoretical structure of the economy. Theory dictated which explanatory variables would be used to explain any given independent variable. During this time, much of the other research into economic fluctuations had a decidedly atheoretic approach. Specifically, the work of Burns and Mitchell (1946) at the NBER focused on measuring various aspects of the business cycle with an eye toward developing economic indicators. These indicators were to be selected on their predictive merits, not their theoretical relevance. Tjalling Koopmans, a leading econometrician at the Cowles Foundation, criticized the Burns-Mitchell approach with his polemic paper "Measurement Without Theory" (1947).

The heyday for econometric modeling occurred in the 1970s in the United States. Advances in computing enabled researchers to run regressions at the touch of a button. Academic institutions, private consulting firms, and the federal government became involved in the development of econometric models. Fundamental procedural problems and criticisms, even those cited by Keynes and Friedman in the early 1940s, remained. These were gruffly pushed aside in the quest to be first and foremost in the blossoming field.

## A Simple Econometric Model

To see how econometric models serve as the basis for forecasts, let us consider a simple example. Assume that the macroeconomic structure of the U.S. economy is summarized by the following equations:

(1) $$C = b1 + b2\ Y;$$

(2) $$I = b3 + b4\ R + b5\ Y_{t-1};$$

(3) $$G = \underline{G};$$

(4) $$Y = C + I + G;$$

Where $C$ is consumer spending; $I$ is business spending; $R$ is the interest rate; $G$ is government spending; and $Y$ is total spending (and also total income).

Equation (4) is known as an "identity" since it merely specifies that total spending in the economy is composed of consumer spending, business spending, and government spending.[8] It is not a regression equation since there are no $b$'s to estimate. Once $C$, $I$, and $G$ are determined, equation (4) states that their sum is equal to total spending in the economy. Moreover, since every penny spent becomes someone's income, $Y$ also represents total income in the cconomy.

Equation (3) is not a regression equation either. It states that government spending is equal to $\underline{G}$, which is whatever number is given for government spending. That is to say, government spending is determined outside the model. Political, not economic, forces determine this number.[9] Its value must be given or guessed to complete the model. Notice that $R$, the value of the interest rate, also must be given in order to figure the level of business spending ($I$).

Equations (1) and (2) reflect how consumer and business spending are determined in the economy. In this context, they are often referred to as "structural" or "behavioral" equations. They actually embody, as we shall see, a bit of economic theory and are regression equations. The $b$'s in them can be determined by ordinary least squares.

Equation (1) states that consumer spending ($C$) depends on the level of income in the economy ($Y$). Keynesian economic theory stipulates that $b2$ be positive but less than unity. That would imply that when income increases, consumer spending increases, but not by as much as the increase in income. Given data for the postwar U.S. economy, ordinary least squares does indeed give such a value for $b2$.

Equation (2) intimates the dependence of business spending on the interest rate ($R$) and income lagged one period ($Y_{t-1}$). Theory indicates that the interest rate has a negative relationship with business spending. High interest rates mean high finance costs and, therefore, less plant and equipment are acquired. Thus, $b4$ is expected to be negative. $b5$, however, should turn out to be positive when estimated. Theoretically, a large increase in spending last period ($Y_{t-1}$) would stimulate production and the need for more plant and equipment this period. In fact, the relationship between business spending and last period's total spending has been given a formal name in economic theory—the accelerator.

You may be thinking that some important variables have been left out of the equations for consumer and business spending. Or you may disagree with the variables (and therefore the theories) that have been used. Perhaps it is overly simplistic to suggest that consumer spending depends upon income and nothing else. What about consumer confidence or interest rates? Are they not important determinants of consumer spending? In economic jargon, we are bickering over the model's "specification." If the equations do not accurately reflect the underlying structure of the economy, then the forecasting performance of the model will be poor.

The model's specification, therefore, is an important issue. No one knows the correct specification with certainty, and there are multitudinous, perhaps infinite, possibilities. This causes one to doubt any particular specification. Furthermore, differently specified models can lead to forecasts that are quite divergent. Keynes made this same critical observation years ago:

> It will be remembered that the seventy translators of the Septuagint were shut up in seventy separate rooms with the Hebrew text and

brought out with them, when they emerged, seventy identical translations. Would the same miracle be vouchsafed if seventy [econometricians] were shut up with the same material? (Keynes, 1940, p. 156)

We now continue with our sample econometric model despite the criticisms, much as the pioneering econometricians did. Once the model is specified, the unknown values in the first two equations ($b1 - b5$) must be estimated. These days, some rather sophisticated techniques are available for this purpose. Ordinary least squares can be applied, but often with biased results. The bias occurs because of "reverse causality" in the regression equations. For example, equation (1) states that consumer spending is determined by income. In reality, income also may be affected by consumer spending: As consumers spend more, producers step up production, and this, in turn, generates more income. In other words, the first equation may have causality running backwards from the dependent variable to the independent variable. Regression analysis assumes that the causality runs from the independent to the dependent variable. If reverse causality is present and ordinary least squares is used to estimate $b1$ and $b2$, then those estimates will be biased.

The amount of bias depends on the degree of reverse causality. In most macroeconomic applications the amount of bias is quite small.[10] On the other hand, one may employ one of the more sophisticated estimation procedures (such as maximum likelihood, described in chapter 5) to avoid the bias entirely.

Once the structural parameters ($b1 - b5$) are estimated, we are in a position to make conditional forecasts with the model. The forecasts are conditional because the values of $R$ (the interest rate) and $G$ (the amount of government spending) must be given in order to solve the model. Suppose that ordinary least squares yielded the following values:

$$b1 = 200;$$
$$b2 = 0.6;$$
$$b3 = 140;$$
$$b4 = -50;$$
$$b5 = 0.2.$$

Let us also suppose that last year's total income was $4,800:

$$Y_{t-1} = 4{,}800.$$

In practice, $b1$–$b5$ and $Y_{t-1}$ are predetermined. $b1$ – $b5$ are determined by the regression analysis and presumably we could look up last year's figure for total income. But we must assume, or be given, values for the interest rate ($R$) and government spending ($G$). Suppose these are:

$$R = 6.0;$$
$$G = 1{,}000.$$

We are now in a position to determine the value for business spending:

$$I = 140 - 50(6.0) + 0.2(4800) = 800.$$

Solving for the values of the remaining two variables of the model, consumer spending ($C$) and total spending ($Y$), is slightly more complicated. But, as you will recall from high school algebra, it can be done because we have two equations and two unknowns:

$$C = 200 + 0.6\ Y;$$
$$Y = C + 800 + 1{,}000.$$

Substituting the first formula into the second gives:

$$Y = 200 + 0.6\ Y + 800 + 1{,}000.$$

Now, solve this for $Y$:

$$Y - 0.6\ Y = 2{,}000;$$

$$0.4\ Y = 2{,}000;$$

$$Y = 2{,}000/0.4 = 5{,}000.$$

Once $Y$ is determined, the value of consumer spending can be obtained:

$$C = 200 + 0.6\ (5{,}000) = 3{,}200.$$

Thus, it is forecast that if the interest rate is 6 percent and government spending equals 1,000, then consumer spending will be 3,200, and business spending will be 800, giving 5,000 for total spending.

This is the manner in which econometric models generate forecasts. Notice that the model produced conditional forecasts for only the variables that were represented by behavioral equations, $C$ and $I$. Regression analysis gave the values for $b1$–$b5$, $Y_{t-1}$ was known beforehand, and values for $R$ and $G$ had to be assumed.

Some of the more obvious criticisms of econometric modeling were, we hope, made evident by this example. The model is unlikely to be specified perfectly. "Reverse causality" in the regression equations of the model can cause biased estimates of the structural parameters (the $b$'s). And, finally, the forecasts are conditional upon the presumed values of the exogenous variables ($R$ and $G$ in our example).

This last criticism is not terribly debilitating since we can solve the model for a variety of values of $R$ and $G$. We might use last year's actual values of these variables or simply try several different estimates. For example, if we used 5.5 percent for $R$ instead of 6.0 percent, the solution of the model yields:

$$I = 825;$$
$$Y = 5,062.5;$$
$$C = 3,237.5.$$

Thus, we can conclude that a lower interest rate will result in more total spending in the economy. Moreover, we can see the specifics of that increase in spending. The half of one percent difference in the interest rate boosts business spending to 825 from 800, while consumer spending rises to 3,237.5 from 3,200. The model is revealing the effects of a decline in the interest rate upon the macroeconomy.

Introductory economics textbooks tell us that an increase in government spending stimulates the economy. Let us see what our model says by changing $G$ to 1,200 from 1,000. Redoing the algebra with this change and resetting the interest rate to 6.0 percent gives:

$$I = 800;$$
$$Y = 5,500;$$
$$C = 3,500.$$

The 200 increase in government spending boosted total spending to 5,500 from 5,000. This implies a government spending multiplier of 2.5—each dollar change in government spending results in a \$2.5 change in total spending. Estimates of the actual government spending multiplier in the United States are slightly lower than this, but this is not bad for a simple model.

## Large-Scale Econometric Models

The econometric model in the previous section was used to demonstrate the fundamental principles of econometric forecasting. The econometric models used by commercial, academic, and government forecasters differ in one respect: They are much larger. State-of-the-art econometric models comprise many more equations and variables. The DRI/McGraw-Hill model of the U.S. economy, which is typical in size, has over 1,000 equations. Over 400 of these are structural.

Modern macroeconometric models are descended from the so-called Klein-Goldberger model developed in the 1950s by Lawrence Klein and Arthur Goldberger.[11] The model consisted of twenty-five equations, ten of which were structural. The model's purpose was the same as Tinbergen's 1940 construction—to evaluate the effects of economic policies and analyze the nature of business cycles. It was not the size or the complexity of the Klein-Goldberger model, but the richness of the economic theory captured in the ten structural equations that set the standard for the next generation of models. The forecasting performance of the Klein-Goldberger model was not exceptionally noteworthy.

The models of the next generation were larger and packed with even more economic theory. A direct descendant of the Klein-Goldberger model was Klein's postwar quarterly model (Klein, 1964). This model was the first to take advantage of the availability of quarterly data over a reasonable time span. Quarterly data are still the preferred frequency of econometricians.

Klein was also involved with the development of the Brookings model.[12] Built under the auspices of the Brookings Institution, the model was huge for its day, with almost 400 equations. This model took advantage of data newly available on a more disaggregated basis. That is to say, for instance, the model included not just one equation for consumer spending, but several—one for consumer spending on vehicles, one for consumer spending on clothing, one for consumer spending on food, and so on. Another interesting aspect of the Brookings model was the nature of its development. It was built using the team approach. Over thirty economists contributed their expertise to the model's construction. Each concentrated on the section of equations corresponding to his or her field of specialization.

Even this prodigious progress was to be surpassed during the heyday of the econometric model—the 1970s. Although the models of the 1960s took advantage of improvements in data, and advances in statistical and economic theory, the 1970s gave rise to the econometric forecasting firm. Advances in the areas just mentioned continued, along with technological progress pertaining to the computer. And the atmosphere was slightly different. It could be perceived that an entire industry was beginning to unfold.

It would be incorrect to attribute the progress in econometrics to competition among the models and modelers. Most of the fledgling models were developed under the sponsorship of academic institutions. Improvements were shared through publications and conferences. Attention became focused, however, on the forecasting prowess of the models. Econometricians became aware of the potential demand, not only for predictions, but also for the economic analysis provided by their systems of equations. Academia did not always provide a suitable environment for competition over clients, so the industry spilled over into the private sector.

This explains the academic lineage of the commercial models. WEFA's model has perhaps the most prestigious genealogy, able to trace its family tree back to the Klein-Goldberger model. But the model used by the Bureau of Economic Analysis in the U.S. Department of Commerce has much of the same ancestry as the WEFA model.

What distinguishes the private forecasting modelers is their attention to the needs of their clients. If a particular client is interested in a forecast of, say, light truck sales, the model can be disaggregated so that spending on light trucks is a separate category within total automotive sales. Now different values for the interest rate, light truck prices, and other truck prices can be plugged in and the model can be solved to procure forecasts for light truck sales. The various scenarios and their corresponding forecasts may be presented to the client in a usable fashion. Private forecasters tailor their models to fit their clients' needs and then present the results in a user-friendly manner.

Private forecasting firms are in competition, to a certain extent, with academic and government-sponsored forecasts. Large corporations pay attention to all of these forecasts. One way to do this is to subscribe to a newsletter such as *Blue Chip Economic Indicators*. This service documents the forecasts of over fifty establishments on a variety of economic variables. We consider this newsletter and the consensus approach to forecasting in the next chapter.

For customized service and detailed economic analysis, clients typically go with a private forecasting firm. But not necessarily. Many of the large brokerage houses have developed their own econometric models with a focus, naturally, on the financial sector of the economy. Regional models are now common. Georgia State's Forecasting Center provides systems of equations for the Southeast United States, the state of Georgia, and the city of Atlanta, aside from its national model. Moreover, the quarterly forecasts are presented at seminars where clients receive, and ask about, economic analysis.

The discussion of large-scale econometric models has been carried out in the context of the United States, but this sort of forecasting is international. Holland has a particularly long and rich history in this field. Econometric models have been developed for many of the nations of the world. It has been recognized that the forecasts from one nation's model can serve as inputs for the models of other nations. This is especially true for countries that are major trading partners. With this idea in mind, Lawrence Klein has devoted much energy and effort to the establishment of "Project Link."[13] As the name suggests, the objective of the project is to connect the national econometric models to result in a global econometric model.

## Vector Autoregressive Models

Two of the biggest pitfalls in econometric modeling are (1) specifying (guessing) the values for the exogenous variables ($G$ and $R$ in our simple example), and (2) deciding what independent variables to include in the behavioral equations, especially when economic theory is ambiguous. These problems are avoided with a technique known as vector autoregressions. Basically, a vector autoregressive model is one that forecasts values for a set of variables using only their own past values.[14] If we wanted to forecast consumer spending (*C*), business spending (*I*), and total spending in the economy (*Y*), as we did with our simple econometric model, we could avoid having to guess at values for the interest rate (*R*) and government spending (*G*). What is more, we could avoid having to consider what factors affect *C*, *I*, and *Y*. Vector autoregressions assume that everything affects everything with a lag:

(5) $$C = b1 + b2\ C_{t-1} + b3\ I_{t-1} + b4\ Y_{t-1} + b5\ Y_{t-2};$$

(6) $$I = b6 + b7\ C_{t-1} + b8\ C_{t-2} + b9\ I_{t-1} + b10\ Y_{t-1};$$

(7) $$Y = b11 + b12\ C_{t-1} + b13\ I_{t-1} + b14\ Y_{t-1}.$$

Equation (5) explains consumer spending with itself lagged once, business spending lagged once, and total spending lagged twice. Equation (6) has business spending depending on consumer spending lagged two periods, with business and total spending lagged one period. And Equation (7) has total spending explained by its own lag and lags of one period on consumer and business spending.

Once it was decided that forecasts for *C*, *I*, and *Y* were required, the only thing that had to be determined was how many lags to use in each case. Some autoregressive models elude even this decision by arbitrarily setting the lag for each variable in each equation to some predetermined length. More often, we need to use trial and error to find lag lengths that work well.[15]

Ordinary least squares can be applied to each equation of the model to find *b*1 through *b*14. Once these values are determined, predictions can be made. Consider equation (5) for consumer spending. To derive a forecast for *C*, simply plug in values for *C* last year (assuming annual data were used to estimate *b*1 – *b*14), last year's *I*, and *Y* from the previous two years. Repeat this procedure for the other two equations to obtain forecasts for *I* and *Y*.

We assess the forecasting accuracy of autoregressive models, and all the techniques outlined in this book, in chapter 8. For now, we can say that vector autoregressive models yield very respectable forecasts, especially considering the simplicity of their design. The drawback of autoregressive forecasting, aside from the more or less arbitrary selection of the lag lengths, is that these models offer no insight into the economics behind their forecasts. In this sense, autoregressive models are like the time-series techniques of the previous chapter—long on statistical procedure, short on economic analysis. If our model were to predict a decline in consumer spending, the only explanation provided is that the previous values of the variables indicate that a drop will occur.

## Summary

Large-scale econometric models of the economy are the predominant method of forecasting in economics today. These models are systems of equations that simulate the economic structure of the nation or region. Each equation represents a piece of the economy. That is to say, it specifies the nature of an economic relationship. It may be the relationship between housing starts and interest rates or the connection between consumer spending and income, or some other economic relation.

These equations have unknown parameters (the $b$'s) that can be estimated using ordinary least squares or some other technique. Once the model is specified and the unknowns are estimated, it can be used to make forecasts.

The major pitfalls in econometric modeling are (1) deciding which variables to include when explaining the behavior of some other variable (i.e., specifying the model correctly), (2) avoiding or correcting for "reverse causality," and (3) determining the values to assume for the exogenous variables of the model in order to make conditional forecasts. These pitfalls cannot be averted entirely. The manner in which they are addressed is what makes econometric forecasting an art.

Vector autoregressive models dodge these pitfalls, but these models bring with them their own set of statistical hazards. In addition, vector autoregressions, like time-series techniques, furnish little in the way of economic explanation for the predictions they generate.

## Notes

1. See Theil (1971, p. 1).
2. Readers interested in these finer details should consult an econometrics textbook, such as Gujarati (1992).

3. See Gujarati (1992, pp. 130–34) for these formulas and their derivations.

4. The predominant test for changes in a relationship over time is known as the Chow test. See Chow (1960).

5. As long as there are more observations than independent variables, ordinary least squares can be applied. However, about thirty more observations than the number of independent variables are preferred.

6. See Tinbergen (1968). This is a reprint of his 1939 work.

7. See Sims (1980) as a starting point for the modern criticisms of econometric modeling.

8. It is assumed that the economy is "closed"—that is, there is no foreign spending (i.e., no imports or exports).

9. This is not completely true. Government spending depends not only on the political process, but also on the state of the economy. As pointed out in chapter 2 (in the context of automatic stabilizers), the amount of welfare spending is determined by the state of the economy. We avoid this complication here in order to keep the example simple.

10. WEFA, the private forecasting firm, uses ordinary least squares to estimate the unknowns in the equations of its large-scale econometric model of the United States. WEFA's founder, Lawrence Klein, feels that the bias caused by reverse causality is small enough to be ignored.

11. See Bodkin, Klein, and Marwah (1991, chapter 3) for an accessible description of the Klein–Goldberger model.

12. See ibid., chapter 4, for a description of the Brookings model.

13. See ibid., chapter 14, for a description of Project Link.

14. This definition is similar to Webb's (1985). Webb's paper is a good starting point for a more detailed investigation into vector autoregressive models.

15. Techniques are available to help select the appropriate lag length in each case. Webb (1985) highlights some of these.

## References

Bodkin, Ronald G.; Klein, Lawrence R.; and Marwah, Kanta. 1991. *A History of Macroeconometric Model-Building.* Brookfield, VT: Edward Elgar.

Burns, Arthur F., and Mitchell, Wesley C. 1946. *Measuring Business Cycles.* New York: NBER.

Chow, Gregory C. 1960. "Tests of Equality between Sets of Coefficients in Two Linear Regressions." *Econometrica* (July): 591–605.

Friedman, Milton. 1940. "Review of Business Cycles in the United States." *American Economic Review,* 30: 657–60.

Gujarati, Damodar. 1992. *Essentials of Econometrics.* New York: McGraw-Hill.

Haberler, Gottfried. 1937. *Prosperity and Depression.* Geneva: League of Nations.

Keynes, John M. 1939. "Professor Tinbergen's Method." *Economic Journal,* 49: 558–68.

———. 1940. "On a Method of Statistical Research: Comment." *Economic Journal,* 50: 154–56.

Klein, Lawrence R. 1964. "A Postwar Quarterly Model: Description and Applications." *Models of Income Determination,* vol. 28 of *Studies in Income and Wealth.* Princeton, NJ: Princeton University Press.

Koopmans, Tjalling C. 1947. "Measurement Without Theory." *Review of Economics and Statistics* (August): 161–72.

Sims, Christopher A. 1980. "Macroeconomics and Reality." *Econometrica,* 48: 1–48.

Theil, Henri. 1971. *Principles of Econometrics.* New York: John Wiley.

Tinbergen, Jan. 1968. *Statistical Testing of Business-Cycle Theories.* New York: Agathon Press.

Webb, Roy H. 1985. "Toward More Accurate Forecasts from Vector Autoregressions." *Economic Review—Federal Reserve Bank of Richmond* (July–August): 3–11.

*7*

# Consensus Forecasts

The best forecasts are made, not by abandoning models or by abandoning judgment, but by blending both sources of information.

—Stephen McNees, 1990

The terms "consensus," "composite," and "combination" generally are used synonymously in forecasting. They refer to the practice of synthesizing two or more forecasts. Sometimes the term "consensus" carries the connotation that some amount of discussion took place and the forecast that emerged was, in some sense, agreed upon by all. This discussion-among-the-experts approach is known as the "Delphi" procedure in business forecasting. It is rarely used in economics, perhaps because economists prefer to disagree than to bow to compromise.

## Introduction

In many instances, it makes good sense not to put all your eggs in one basket. This simple idea is the primary reason for selecting a combination forecast over any single forecast. The benefits achieved from using a consensus of forecasts are very similar to the benefits derived from diversifying an investment portfolio. There will always be individual stocks that outperform an expanded portfolio, but what are the odds that you will pick the outperformer? A diversified portfolio of investments results in decreased volatility, and therefore, more return for any given amount of risk.

Techniques for combining forecasts will be presented shortly. For now, it is interesting to note that simply averaging together the individual forecasts works about as well as any combining strategy. Theoretically speaking, it would be better to combine forecasts that were generated by different forecasting procedures. For instance, more stands to be gained from blending an ARIMA forecast with a forecast from an econometric model than from the combination of two forecasts from econometric models, since the different techniques consider dissimilar information. The combination of forecasts that synthesizes more information should be more accurate.

On the other hand, econometric models can be disparate enough that their combination succeeds in blending distinct information. Furthermore, there is some evidence that combining several of the same type of forecasts, especially time-series forecasts, works well.[1] There are benefits to be gained from the amalgamation of forecasts regardless of their origin.

## Consensus Forecasts

These ideas explain why many firms subscribe to several forecasting services. They like to see where their favorite forecast stands relative to the others. This sort of informal combining is common. If you have a forecast of real GDP, the thirty-year Treasury bond rate, the inflation rate, or the unemployment rate, why not pick up *Economic Times* (a monthly publication of the Conference Board) and see what other forecasters are predicting. Many daily and weekly business publications report a consensus forecast for economic variables as the release date for the figure approaches.

Often this consensus figure is obtained from a firm in Sedona, Arizona, called Blue Chip Economic Indicators, Inc. (BCEI). Begun in 1976 and run by Robert Eggert, BCEI polls about fifty economic forecasters each month. The respondents provide forecasts on as many as fifteen different economic variables and this does not include the special questions that are asked concerning a variety of economic events. BCEI averages together all the forecasts to provide the consensus forecast and also notes which forecasts have been revised. A diffusion index from the upward and downward revisions is calculated. The BCEI newsletter is widely disseminated and well respected.

Other establishments also track and combine economic forecasts. Beginning in 1946, the business writer Joseph A. Livingston conducted biannual surveys of economic forecasters. For many years, his survey was

Table 7.1

**Blue Chip Economic Indicators and Naive Forecasts of GDP Growth**

| Year | Actual GDP growth (percent) | BCEI consensus forecast (percent) | Error | Naive forecast (percent)[a] | Error |
|------|------|------|------|------|------|
| 1977 | 4.7 | 4.9 | +0.2 | 4.9 | +0.2 |
| 1978 | 5.3 | 4.3 | −1.0 | 4.7 | −0.6 |
| 1979 | 2.5 | 2.7 | +0.2 | 5.3 | +2.8 |
| 1980 | −0.2 | −0.2 | 0.0 | 2.5 | +2.7 |
| 1981 | 1.9 | 0.9 | −1.0 | −0.2 | −2.1 |
| 1982 | −2.5 | 2.2 | +4.7 | 1.9 | +4.4 |
| 1983 | 3.6 | 3.2 | −0.4 | −2.5 | −6.1 |
| 1984 | 6.4 | 5.1 | −1.3 | 3.6 | −2.8 |
| 1985 | 2.7 | 3.5 | +0.8 | 6.4 | +3.7 |
| 1986 | 2.5 | 3.1 | +0.6 | 2.7 | +0.2 |
| Average absolute error | | | 1.0 | | 2.6 |

*Source*: Blue Chip Economic Indicators, Inc.
[a]The naive forecast assumes the current year's growth rate will be equal to last year's growth rate.

the state of the art in tracking economic forecasts. Livingston's survey has been taken over by the Federal Reserve Bank of Philadelphia.

In a joint endeavor, the American Statistical Association and the NBER have kept a compilation of forecasts from a large number of economic forecasters. Victor Zarnowitz was the main compiler and analyzer of these forecasts. Again, the Federal Reserve Bank of Philadelphia now maintains the American Statistical Association–NBER survey.

And finally, the Conference Board, through the above-mentioned *Economic Times,* keeps tabs on about a dozen of the major forecasting establishments.

It is interesting to consider that almost all of the major economic forecasting establishments use several forecasting techniques and combine them, in some fashion, to arrive at the figure they submit to BCEI. What does it mean to combine combination forecasts? One would not expect a large improvement in forecast accuracy since the information from a variety of techniques is already in the individual forecasts.

Nevertheless, the predictive accuracy of BCEI is noteworthy. Table 7.1 compares the BCEI consensus forecast and a "naive" forecast with the actual GDP data.

The naive forecast, which assumes that last period's growth rate will prevail in the next period, is a straw man that should easily be improved upon. The BCEI consensus beats it handily, with an average absolute error of 1.0, compared with 2.6. The absolute value of the errors is taken before averaging to prohibit the negative errors (overestimates) from canceling out the positive errors (underestimates). Forecasts can be quite inaccurate and still average out to near zero unless the absolute value of the prediction errors is taken.

Notice that the BCEI consensus is not infallible. The consensus missed calling the recession that began in July 1981 and lasted until November 1982. Turning points, especially cyclical peaks, are difficult to foresee with any technique and, thus, difficult for the consensus to predict.

Further evaluation of consensus forecasting will be taken up in the next chapter. For right now, it simply is noted that consensus forecasting is philosophically sound, increasingly popular, and there is ample evidence that it enhances accuracy. Great. But are there not some forecasters who are consistently better than average? The answer to that question, according to Victor Zarnowitz (1984), is yes. His analysis of the American Statistical Association–NBER consensus forecasts revealed a small group of forecasters who were superior. But a similar study, by Stephen McNees (1987), advises caution. Working with the BCEI consensus, McNees confirms Zarnowitz's results but also finds that different forecasters are better at predicting different economic variables. Not only that, some forecasters are superior at short-run predictions, while others perform better when forecasting further into the future. Because of these complications, it is very difficult to select forecasting establishments that are superior overall. It depends on which variable is to be forecasted for what length of time.

## Methods for Combining Forecasts

It is tempting to combine economic forecasts using the same method used to combine judges' scores at a diving competition: throw out the high and the low scores and average the others together. In economic forecasting, the extreme forecasts are not thrown out. Indeed, the diversity of the individual predictions only serves to enhance the consensus forecast. If all the predictions were just about the same, the combination could not possibly be much of an improvement.

In diving, the radical scores may be the result of a bad viewing angle or a prejudicial bias. As we shall see in the next chapter, an economic forecast is not considered biased unless it consistently over- or under-predicts its target over time. An extreme forecast is not necessarily biased.

It may be asserted that some forecasters have a poor perspective on the economy, just as some diving judges have a bad poolside angle. But suppose one of these forecasters, or diving judges, saw something, some flaw, from his or her angle that was imperceptible to others. The subsequent divergent forecast, or score, would be a valuable addition to the consensus.

Thus, one method for combining forecasts in economics is to average together *all* of the individual forecasts. This is the method adopted by BCEI and the American Statistical Association–NBER consensus.

A variation of this method is to average the individual predictions together but give more weight to the superior forecasters. It was noted in the previous section that it is difficult to identify which forecasters, and therefore which forecasts, are better. In practice, this may be overcome with some selection gauge. For instance, we may give more weight to those forecasts that have been more accurate in the immediate past.

There are many other possibilities. One of these, which we shall investigate, is to employ a regression analysis to determine the weight to give to each of the individual forecasts. Let us use each of these methods to combine some forecasts of real GDP.

Table 7.2 gives three sets of forecasts for the quarterly growth rates of real GDP from the first quarter of 1992 (1992.1) to the first quarter of 1995 (1995.1).

As before, the naive forecast assumes that the growth rate of GDP this quarter will be the same as last. The ARIMA forecast is based on a time-series model with three autoregressive terms and three moving-average terms. The data were differenced to achieve stationarity. The econometric forecast is that of the Georgia State University Forecasting Center. Table 7.3 gives the errors for each set of forecasts.

At least for this period of time, the econometric model is the most accurate. The average absolute forecast error is lowest for these forecasts. The ARIMA model is a close second, while the naive forecast, our straw man, trails.

Let us see if forecast accuracy can be improved by combining the sets of forecasts. As mentioned, there are several methods for blending individual forecasts. Table 7.4 gives three sets of combination forecasts

Table 7.2

## Quarterly Real GDP Growth and Forecasts

| Date | Actual GDP growth (percent) | Naive forecast (percent) | ARIMA forecast (percent) | Econometric forecast (percent) |
|------|------|------|------|------|
| 1992.1 | 3.1 | 0.1 | 0.9 | 0.7 |
| 1992.2 | 2.4 | 3.1 | 2.4 | 2.4 |
| 1992.3 | 3.5 | 2.4 | 2.6 | 1.6 |
| 1992.4 | 5.7 | 3.5 | 2.4 | 2.8 |
| 1993.1 | 1.2 | 5.7 | 3.9 | 2.6 |
| 1993.2 | 2.4 | 1.2 | 2.2 | 3.6 |
| 1993.3 | 2.7 | 2.4 | 1.7 | 5.2 |
| 1993.4 | 6.3 | 2.7 | 2.8 | 3.5 |
| 1994.1 | 3.3 | 6.3 | 4.0 | 2.5 |
| 1994.2 | 4.1 | 3.3 | 2.8 | 4.1 |
| 1994.3 | 4.0 | 4.1 | 3.2 | 3.5 |
| 1994.4 | 5.1 | 4.0 | 2.9 | 3.5 |
| 1995.1 | 2.8 | 5.1 | 3.7 | 3.5 |

*Source*: Department of Commerce, *Economic Times,* and author's calculations.

Table 7.3

## Forecast Errors[a]

| Date | Naive forecast error | ARIMA recast error | Econometric forecast error |
|------|------|------|------|
| 1992.1 | 3.0 | 2.2 | 2.4 |
| 1992.2 | −0.7 | 0.0 | 0.0 |
| 1992.3 | 1.1 | 0.9 | 1.9 |
| 1992.4 | 2.2 | 3.3 | 2.9 |
| 1993.1 | −4.5 | −2.7 | −1.4 |
| 1993.2 | 1.2 | 0.2 | −1.2 |
| 1993.3 | 0.3 | 1.0 | −2.5 |
| 1993.4 | 3.6 | 3.5 | 2.8 |
| 1994.1 | −3.0 | −0.7 | 0.8 |
| 1994.2 | 0.8 | 1.3 | 0.0 |
| 1994.3 | −0.1 | 0.8 | 0.5 |
| 1994.4 | 1.1 | 2.2 | 1.6 |
| 1995.1 | 0.8 | −0.9 | −0.7 |
| Average absolute error | 1.72 | 1.52 | 1.44 |

*Source*: U.S. Department of Commerce, *Economic Times,* and author's calculations.
[a]Forecast errors are equal to the actual value minus the forecast

Table 7.4

**Combination Forecasts and Their Errors**

| Date | Equal weights (percent) | Error | Performance weights (percent) | Error | Regression weights (percent) | Error |
|---|---|---|---|---|---|---|
| 1992.1 | 0.6 | 2.5 | 0.6 | 2.5 | 3.4 | −0.3 |
| 1992.2 | 2.6 | −0.2 | 2.6 | −0.2 | 3.5 | −1.1 |
| 1992.3 | 2.2 | 1.3 | 2.2 | 1.3 | 3.5 | 0.0 |
| 1992.4 | 2.9 | 2.8 | 2.9 | 2.8 | 3.5 | 2.2 |
| 1993.1 | 4.1 | −2.9 | 4.0 | −2.8 | 3.3 | −2.1 |
| 1993.2 | 2.3 | 0.1 | 2.4 | 0.0 | 4.0 | −1.6 |
| 1993.3 | 3.1 | −0.4 | 3.2 | −0.5 | 4.0 | −1.3 |
| 1993.4 | 3.0 | 3.3 | 3.0 | 3.3 | 3.8 | 2.5 |
| 1994.1 | 4.3 | −1.0 | 4.1 | −0.8 | 3.2 | 0.1 |
| 1994.2 | 3.4 | 0.7 | 3.4 | 0.7 | 3.8 | 0.3 |
| 1994.3 | 3.6 | 0.4 | 3.6 | 0.4 | 3.6 | 0.4 |
| 1994.4 | 3.5 | 1.6 | 3.4 | 1.7 | 3.6 | 1.5 |
| 1995.1 | 4.1 | −1.3 | 4.0 | −1.2 | 3.5 | −0.7 |
| Average absolute error | | 1.42 | | 1.40 | | 1.08 |

*Source*: U.S. Department of Commerce, *Economic Times,* and author's calculations.

and the errors for each set. The "equal weights" forecast is the simple average of all three individual forecasts. The "performance weights" forecast gives more weight to the ARIMA and econometric forecasts because those are more accurate. The "regression weights" forecast combines the three individual forecasts based on a regression analysis.

Notice that all three combination forecasts have average absolute errors that are lower than those for any individual forecast. For quarterly real GDP growth rates from 1992.1 to 1995.1, any combination forecast is superior to any individual set of forecasts. Moreover, the combination method that works best is when the weights are determined by regression analysis. Let us take a detailed look at how each combination forecast was generated.

### Combining Forecasts with Equal Weights

Simply averaging together individual predictions is the industry standard for generating consensus forecasts. When a simple average is taken, each prediction gets the same weight, or importance, in the determination of the average. The "equal weights" forecasts in Table 7.4 were obtained by averaging together the three individual forecasts for each quarter. For 1992.1 the individual forecasts were 0.1 percent (naive), 0.9 percent (ARIMA), and 0.7 percent (econometric). The average of these three values, 0.6 percent, is reported as the equal weights forecast for 1992.1.

This combining method avoids having to select which forecasts are better. It takes the good with the bad and uses the diversity of the individual forecasts to create an amalgam of equally blended parts. Notice, however, that of the three combining methods reported in Table 7.4, this one results in the highest average absolute error.

### Combining Forecasts with Performance Weights

Another method for combining forecasts is to take a weighted average of the individual forecasts. Forecasts that are, in some sense, better are given more weight. One may, quite simply, give more credence to the econometric forecast because of its sophistication relative to the other techniques. Or the most accurate forecast over some sample period may be given more leverage in the combined forecast.

This is what was done to obtain the "performance forecasts" in Table 7.4. The econometric forecast was given the most weight because it had the lowest average absolute error over the sample period. The naive predictions were given the least influence in the combined forecast because of their relatively high average absolute error.

Very specifically, the reciprocals of the average absolute errors for each type of forecast were summed together. This gave 1.93 (= 1/1.72 + 1/1.52 + 1/1.44). Then each reciprocal was divided by this sum. Thus, 1/1.72 divided by 1.92 gives 0.30 or 30 percent. This is the weight given to the naive forecasts. The weight given to the ARIMA predictions is 1/1.52 divided by 1.93, which equals 0.34 or 34 percent. Finally, the weight given to the econometric forecasts is 1/1.44 divided by 1.93, 0.36 or 36 percent. Notice that the three weights, 0.30, 0.34, and 0.36, sum to unity. Had they not, because of rounding, they would have to be adjusted so that they would. One hundred percent of the combined forecast must be determined by the individual forecasts.

Once the three weights are determined, the "performance-weighted" combined forecasts are easily derived. Each type of forecast is multiplied by its weight and the three products are summed together. For 1992.1, the calculation was:

(0.3)0.1 percent + (0.34)0.9 percent + (0.36)0.7 percent = 0.6 percent.

In Table 7.4, the performance-weighted forecasts had a lower average absolute error than the equally weighted combination. This is to be expected since more credence was placed on the type of forecasts that had lower errors. But there is no guarantee that the performance-weighted forecasts will outperform the equally weighted forecasts in the future.

### Combining Forecasts with Regression Weights

The "regression weights" forecasts presented in Table 7.4 were derived by combining the three sets of forecasts with weights determined by a regression of the actual growth rates of GDP on the predictions:

$$GDP = b1 + b2 \ NAIVE + b3 \ ARIMA + b4 \ ECONO,$$

where *GDP* is the actual growth rate of real GDP; *NAIVE* is the naive forecast of real GDP growth; *ARIMA* is the ARIMA model's forecast of real GDP growth; *ECONO* is the econometric model's forecast of real GDP growth.

Applying ordinary least squares to the data from 1992.1 to 1995.1 gives the following values for $b1$ through $b4$:

$$b1 = 3.18;$$
$$b2 = -0.16;$$
$$b3 = 0.14;$$
$$b4 = 0.19.$$

To obtain the combination forecast for 1992.1, simply plug in the individual forecasts from that quarter and these parameter estimates:

$$GDP = 3.18 - 0.16 \ (0.1) + 0.14 \ (0.9) + 0.19 \ (0.7) = 3.4 \ percent.$$

Notice that the weights determined by the regression analysis, $-.16$, 0.14, and 0.19, do not sum to unity. And the weight given to the naive forecast is negative! These peculiarities, however, are not liabilities of this weighting procedure. It is possible to restrict the parameter estimates, $b2$–$b3$, to sum to unity and $b1$ to equal zero. Indeed, this is yet another variation on determining the weights when combining forecasts. It can also be stipulated that none of the weights be negative. However, Granger and Ramanathan (1984) have demonstrated that the unrestricted version of the procedure presented here is often superior. Moreover, these authors have shown that the combination forecasts developed from the unrestricted regression will be unbiased even if the individual forecasts being combined are biased.

There are no justifiable benefits to restricting the regression coefficients in any fashion when forming combination forecasts with this approach. Therefore, we will not concern ourselves with exactly how these sorts of restrictions can be implemented.[2]

### The Role of Judgment and Adjustments

It would be extremely unusual for a professional forecaster in economics to promulgate a prediction fresh from the computer without adjusting it. This is especially true with regard to the forecasts generated by large-scale econometric models. You may recall from chapter 6 that these models require assumed values for some variables in order to make predictions for the others. Judgment comes into play when deciding what values to experiment with and which resulting forecast to rely on. Even after this, forecasts may be adjusted to correspond with current events that the model does not explicitly consider.

Remember that trend extrapolation, ARIMA forecasts, and vector autoregressions rely solely on statistical procedures. These predictions may be adjusted to conform with an economic analysis of current or expected future events. More often, the forecasts generated with these techniques are used to help in adjusting econometric forecasts. Looked at this way, combination forecasting is a form of adjustment. Econometric forecasts are adjusted when they are combined with other types of predictions. And judgment is necessary to make combination forecasts. What forecasts are to be combined? What weighting procedure will be used?

The manner in which economic forecasts are adjusted is not formalized. Although some professionals may use a formal combination procedure, most do not. Even these established adjustment procedures are liable to be altered in certain circumstances. In the end, it is the style and grace forecasters exhibit in the adjustment process that distinguishes them. The best economic forecasting houses use all the techniques described in this book: large-scale econometric models, trend extrapolation, ARIMA models, vector autoregressions, economic indicators, business-cycle analysis, and perhaps even wave theory. Trained econometricians and computer scientists are going to be needed to ply these techniques. But somewhere along the line there is an "artist" who takes what these procedures give and creates a forecast and analysis that allow the client to make a better business decision.

### McNees's Study

There is some evidence, however, that economic forecasters are going too far in refining the raw predictions generated by their statistical procedures. This is the conclusion of Stephen McNees, a researcher at the Federal Reserve Bank of New England.[3] Indeed, his authoritative study of the adjustment of economic forecasts makes several interesting points.

First, McNees compared the adjusted forecasts from four prominent large-scale econometric models with those from an unadjusted ARIMA modeling procedure. The results: With very few exceptions, the adjusted econometric forecasts were more accurate than the unadjusted ARIMA predictions.

It was a closer race between the adjusted forecasts of the econometric modelers and the unadjusted forecasts from a vector autoregressive model. But the adjusted macroeconometric forecasts won again when the vector autoregressive technique broke down in the late 1980s.

After this, McNees is not ready to conclude that adjustments improve the accuracy of economic forecasts. It could be that the econometric models are superior to the ARIMA and the vector autoregressive models and that is why the predictions of the former are more accurate. In other words, it may be that the econometric models outperform the other techniques despite the fact that the econometric forecasts are adjusted.

To overcome this concern, McNees obtained both the adjusted and the unadjusted forecasts from a group of econometric modelers. Now the adjusted and unadjusted forecasts from the exact same models could be compared. In a phrase, the finding was that the adjustments enhanced forecast accuracy. But that conclusion needs to be tempered. First, the adjustments were more helpful in improving short-term forecasts. When making predictions for up to two years into the future, judgmental revisions were not as beneficial as they were in refining forecasts of the immediate future.

Second, the unadjusted forecasts were more reliable when it came to predicting three specific variables: imports, the prices of imports, and the change in business inventories. McNees suggests that judgmental revisions work best when new, more reliable data on a particular variable become available to guide the direction and magnitude of the adjustment. This would be the case with a variable such as short-term interest rates. A forecaster could look and see where those rates stand right now. That will help a great deal in revising the forecast given by the model. Furthermore, the figure the forecaster sees for short-term interest rates today is not going to be revised. For the three instances where adjustments do not help (imports, import prices, and inventory changes), data updates are not available on a timely basis or the updates are likely to be widely revised in the future.

So if we are buying a short-term prediction of an economic variable other than the three cited immediately above, we will want it to be adjusted in line with the judgment of the forecaster. Again, it is these adjustments that distinguish the projections of the various large-scale econometric models of the U.S. economy.

But the final lesson to be drawn from McNees's study is that, in practice, the alterations to the models' forecasts are overdone. He finds that, had the four forecasters in his study placed more weight on the purely econometric projections and less on their modifications, their forecasts would have been still more accurate.

## Summary

This chapter has pointed out the benefits of consensus forecasting. It is easily done and most likely will improve accuracy. Commercial establishments, such as Blue Chip Economic Indicators, and other organizations, such as the Federal Reserve Bank of Philadelphia, track the individual predictions of economic forecasters and average them together to form the consensus forecast.

Simple averaging, however, is not the only method for combining forecasts. Two of the many other possibilities have been presented here: (1) taking a weighted average of the individual forecasts where the weights are based on previous accuracy, and (2) using regression analysis to form the consensus prediction.

Another issue considered in this chapter is the role of judgment in adjusting the forecasts generated by the various statistical procedures in use today. Since the major forecasting houses rely primarily on large-scale econometric models and secondarily on the other techniques (ARIMA, economic indicators, and vector autoregressions), their prognostications differ because of the manner in which these various forecasts are combined. To put it another way, the forecasted values derived from the econometric models must be tempered by the results of the other forecasting techniques and adjusted in light of current events. Generally speaking, these adjustments enhance the accuracy of the forecasts.

This approach—large-scale econometric forecasts combined with predictions from other techniques and discretely adjusted according to the judgment of the forecaster—is the state of the art in economic forecasting today.

## Notes

1. See Winkler (1984).
2. The interested reader may consult Gujarati (1992, pp. 404–9).
3. See McNees (1990).

## References

Granger, C.W.J., and Ramanathan, Ramu. 1984. "Improved Methods of Combining Forecasts." *Journal of Forecasting,* 3: 197–204.

Gujarati, Damodar. 1992. *Essentials of Econometrics.* New York: McGraw-Hill.

McNees, Stephen K. 1987. "Consensus Forecasts: Tyranny of the Majority." *New England Economic Review* (November–December): 15–21.

———. 1990. "The Role of Judgment in Macroeconomic Forecasting Accuracy." *International Journal of Forecasting* (October): 287–99.

Winkler, Robert L. 1984. "Combining Forecasts." In Spyros Makridakis, et al. (ed.), *The Forecasting Accuracy of Major Time-Series Methods.* New York: John Wiley, pp. 292–311.

Zarnowitz, Victor. 1984. "The Accuracy of Individual and Group Forecasts from Business Outlook Surveys." *Journal of Forecasting* (January–March): 11–26.

# 8

# Evaluation of Economic Forecasts

> Assuming that the forecasts have been prepared for some decision
> purpose, we can say that their quality is determined by the
> quality of the decision to which they led.
>
> —Henri Theil, 1966

Economic forecasters certainly have taken their share of criticism over the years. In this chapter we shall see if they deserve to be reproached. Is the accuracy of economic forecasts wanting? Is it improving? Is bias detected in any of the forecasts? Which forecasting technique is most reliable?

Clear-cut responses to questions such as these are elusive. Take the last query, concerning the reliability of the various techniques. As it turns out, some techniques are more reliable than others for certain variables. And some forecasting methods work better in the short run, while others have a better track record making forecasts years in advance.

There are no universally correct answers to questions involving forecast performance. Forecasts can be evaluated, however, for given circumstances. We shall see which technique is best in this situation or that. This is part of the art of forecasting—knowing the limits of various methods under diverse conditions.

## Forecast Accuracy

There are enough ways to measure forecast accuracy that we certainly do not want to review them all. Different measures of accuracy do not always concur. But typically, the sundry measures will result in the same appraisal. Here are a handful of the most useful gauges of forecast accuracy.

### Average Absolute Error

With all the measures of forecast accuracy, different analysts, and different textbooks, will use an unsettling variety of names for the exact same measurement device. The average absolute error (AAE) frequently is referred to as the mean absolute deviation, or the mean absolute error. One can imagine the other possibilities. In any case, what we shall call the AAE is the average of the forecast errors, over some time period, after taking the absolute value of those errors.

Let us define the forecast error in period $t$ to be:

$$e_t = X_t - FX_t,$$

where $X_t$ is the actual value in period $t$ and $FX_t$ is the forecasted value.

Then the AAE is:

$$AAE = \frac{\Sigma |e_t|}{n}$$

where $n$ is the number of forecast errors.

We have already used this criterion in chapter 7 to demonstrate the sharper accuracy of combined forecasts relative to the individual forecasts that comprise the combination. Taking the absolute value of the forecast errors ensures that the negative errors (overestimates) do not offset the positive errors (underestimates).

### Root Average Squared Error

Another way of getting around the problem of the negative errors offsetting the positive ones is to square them. The negative forecast errors become positive when squared. These squared values are averaged together and then the square root is taken in order to rescale that average to its original dimension.

We call this statistic the root average squared error (RASE). Elsewhere, it is referred to as the root mean squared deviation, or root mean squared error. In mathematical terms:

Table 8.1

**Hypothetical Forecasts and Errors**

| Data($X_t$) | Forecast 1($FX1_t$) | Error 1($e1_t$) | Forecast 2($FX2_t$) | Error 2($e2_t$) |
|---|---|---|---|---|
| 3.0 | 2.5 | −0.5 | 3.0 | 0.0 |
| 4.0 | 4.5 | 0.5 | 4.0 | 0.0 |
| 5.0 | 4.5 | −0.5 | 5.0 | 0.0 |
| 6.0 | 6.5 | 0.5 | 8.0 | −2.0 |
| | | AAE = 0.5 | | AAE = 0.5 |
| | | RASE = 0.5 | | RASE = 1.0 |

$$RASE = \sqrt{\frac{\Sigma e_i^2}{n}}$$

Table 8.1 contains hypothetical data and forecasts in order to demonstrate the calculation of the RASE and contrast the results with the AAE.

Notice that the AAE is the same for both sets of forecast errors. Thus, according to the AAE, both sets of predictions are equally accurate. But the RASE is lower for the first set of forecasts. According to the RASE, the first set of forecasts is more accurate. It has the lower RASE.

The difference between the two accuracy criteria is that the RASE penalizes heavily for large forecast errors. The second set of forecasts is perfectly accurate until the last prediction where a relatively large error (−2.0) is made. The first set of forecasts makes four smaller errors that sum (in absolute value) to the same magnitude as the one large error in the second set. The AAE cannot distinguish between the two cases and rates them evenly. The RASE, on the other hand, favors the first set of forecasts where several small errors are made, as opposed to one large error.

The decision about which of these two criteria to use in practice depends upon the preference of the analyst. If the choice is to highlight large forecast errors, then the RASE should be used. Again, in practice, all of the accuracy measures presented here typically will rank the sets of forecasts in the same order.

### Average Absolute Percentage Error

Yet another accuracy gauge is the average absolute percentage error

(AAPE). This measure, as its name suggests, considers the errors in percentage terms. To calculate the AAPE:

$$AAPE = \frac{\sum \frac{|e_t|}{X_t}}{n}$$

The AAPE is especially useful for comparing forecasts of variables that are of different magnitude. In a sense, it is never fair to compare forecasts for different variables. Some economic phenomena are more erratic and, therefore, more difficult to predict with precision. For instance, forecasting real GDP is less precarious than predicting long-term interest rates.

It also would be inequitable to compare forecasts of variables that differed in magnitude. As an example, forecasts of government spending would be considered poor if they had errors that exceeded $125 billion. But an error of $125 billion on a forecast for consumer spending is quite acceptable. This is because $125 billion is nearly 10 percent of government spending, while it is only approximately 2 percent of consumer spending.

The AAPE allows for a more proper comparison when the forecasts are for variables that differ widely in size. Table 8.2 demonstrates this point by comparing the AAE and the AAPE for two sets of hypothetical predictions where one variable is ten times the size of the other.

The AAE clearly signals the first set of forecasts to be more accurate with a reading of 0.5 compared with 5.0 for the second set. But the second set of forecasts is identical to the first except that the data are blown up by a factor of ten. The AAPE takes this into consideration and gives both sets of forecasts the same score for accuracy, 0.12. This indicates that the typical forecast is off by 12 percent in this example.

Caution is required when comparing forecasts for variables that differ in magnitude. Forecast errors can appear to be large in absolute terms when they are actually quite reasonable in percentage terms. On the other hand, some economic phenomena are more difficult to predict and result in forecast errors that are, indeed, relatively large. The AAPE is the appropriate statistic to gauge forecast accuracy under these sorts of circumstances.

Table 8.2

**Hypothetical Forecasts and Errors**

| Data 1($X1_t$) | Forecast 1($FX1_t$) | Error 1($e1_t$) | Data 2($X2_t$) | Forecast 2($FX_t$) | Error 2($e2_t$) |
|---|---|---|---|---|---|
| 3.0 | 2.5 | −0.5 | 30 | 25 | −5.0 |
| 4.0 | 4.5 | 0.5 | 40 | 45 | 5.0 |
| 5.0 | 4.5 | −0.5 | 50 | 45 | −5.0 |
| 6.0 | 6.5 | 0.5 | 60 | 65 | 5.0 |
| | | AAE = 0.5 | | | AAE = 5.0 |
| | | AAPE = 0.12 | | | AAPE = 0.12 |

## *Theil's Coefficient of Inequality*

The last statistic for gauging forecast accuracy to be presented here is
Theil's coefficient of inequality. We will refer to this statistic as "$U$"
since Theil himself uses that designation.[1] There are several versions
of $U$. Confusingly, they all go by the same name. The version given
here seems to be the most common.

$$U = \frac{RASE}{\sqrt{\frac{\sum FX_t^2}{n}} + \sqrt{\frac{\sum X_t^2}{n}}}.$$

Although Theil's $U$ is a bit more obscure than the AAE, the RASE,
or the AAPE, it is extremely useful. Like the AAPE, $U$ has a sense of
proportion and will score forecast errors in relation to the magnitude of
the variable being predicted. For the two sets of forecasts in Table 8.2,
Theil's $U$ is equivalent (0.05). And like RASE, $U$ considers one large
forecast error to be more inaccurate than a lot of small errors that sum
(in absolute value) to the same amount as the large error. Thus, in
Table 8.1, $U = 0.05$ for the first set of forecast errors and $U = 0.10$ for
the second set, which contains the one large error. Therefore, $U$ is an
appropriate gauge of accuracy in a wide range of situations.

Let us tie together all four measures of forecast accuracy in one
example. This is done in Table 8.3, where three sets of forecasts of the
interest rate on thirty-year Treasury bonds are presented along with the
actual rates from the first quarter of 1992 to the last quarter of 1994.

Table 8.3

**Actual Forecasts and Errors for the Thirty-Year Treasury Bond Interest Rate**

| Date | 30-year rate | Fore-cast 1 | Error 1 | Fore-cast 2 | Error 2 | Fore-cast 3 | Error 3 |
|------|------|------|------|------|------|------|------|
| 1992.1 | 7.7 | 7.8 | −0.1 | 7.7 | 0.0 | 7.2 | 0.5 |
| 1992.2 | 7.8 | 7.7 | 0.1 | 7.7 | 0.1 | 8.0 | −0.2 |
| 1992.3 | 7.2 | 7.8 | 0.6 | 7.8 | −0.6 | 7.5 | −0.3 |
| 1992.4 | 7.3 | 7.2 | 0.1 | 7.1 | 0.2 | 8.0 | −0.7 |
| 1993.1 | 6.9 | 7.3 | −0.4 | 7.4 | −0.5 | 7.5 | −0.6 |
| 1993.2 | 6.6 | 6.9 | −0.3 | 6.8 | −0.2 | 6.9 | −0.3 |
| 1993.3 | 6.2 | 6.6 | −0.4 | 6.6 | −0.4 | 6.6 | −0.4 |
| 1993.4 | 6.1 | 6.2 | −0.1 | 6.1 | 0.0 | 6.1 | 0.0 |
| 1994.1 | 6.5 | 6.1 | 0.4 | 6.2 | 0.3 | 6.3 | 0.2 |
| 1994.2 | 7.4 | 6.5 | 0.9 | 6.6 | 0.8 | 6.7 | 0.7 |
| 1994.3 | 7.7 | 7.4 | 0.3 | 7.6 | 0.1 | 7.3 | 0.4 |
| 1994.4 | 8.1 | 7.7 | 0.4 | 7.7 | 0.4 | 8.0 | 0.1 |
| | | | | | | | |
| AAE | | | 0.324 | | 0.298 | | 0.365 |
| RASE | | | 0.405 | | 0.377 | | 0.424 |
| AAPE | | | 4.582 | | 4.249 | | 5.118 |
| $U$ | | | 0.028 | | 0.026 | | 0.030 |

*Source*: U.S. Department of Commerce, *Economic Times,* author's calculations.

Forecast 1 is the "naive" forecast. It predicts the interest rate this quarter to be what it was last quarter. Forecast 2 is derived from an ARIMA model. In this particular case, one autoregressive term was used to predict the interest rate. The data first had to be differenced to achieve stationarity. There were no moving-average terms employed in this ARIMA model. The third set of forecasts, Forecast 3, is from Wharton Econometric Forecasting Associates (WEFA). They, of course, employ a large-scale econometric model and adjust the predictions from the model along the lines discussed in the previous chapter.

First, let it be known that long-term interest rates, such as the thirty-year Treasury bond rate, are notoriously difficult to forecast. AAEs and RASEs below 0.5 are quite respectable for one-quarter-ahead forecasts. The AAPEs, which range from 4.2 to 5.1, indicate that these forecasts are typically off by about 4 percent to 5 percent.

All four accuracy measures concur that the ARIMA model gives the most precise forecasts over this sample period and the naive predictions outperform those of WEFA. A word in WEFA's defense: Their forecasts of the thirty-year bond rate were made early in the quarter. The revisions made to these forecasts as more information became available are likely to have improved their accuracy.

### Turning Point Analysis

The predictions given in Table 8.3 cover the period from early 1992 to the end of 1994. During this time, the U.S. economy was in a continuous expansionary phase of the business cycle. It is likely that the forecasts would have been less accurate had the economy experienced a "turning point" during the period. If the economy had shifted phases of the business cycle, or if only the bond market had passed from a bull to a bear market, the forecasts would have had more of a challenge. After all, it is reasonable to assume that the current environment will continue to exist and to make predictions accordingly. It is extremely hazardous, however, to predict that there will be an abrupt change in a specific quarter. Turning points in economic activity often catch forecasters unaware.

Because of this difficulty, another way to assess economic predictions is to note when, and if, they signaled turning points. A 1987 study of both individual and consensus forecasts suggests there is much room for improvement on this score.[2] The study points out that the forecasters did not recognize the onset of the 1973 and 1982 recessions until about the time that they began. Warnings of the brief 1980 recession came early, but the exact quarter of its commencement was, again, only recognized as the recession got underway. Keep in mind that some credit is due for being able to identify turning points as they occur. The NBER Business Cycle Dating Committee does not declare the peaks and troughs in economic activity until well after the fact. It would be impressive if an economic forecaster could predict turning points in the business cycle one quarter in advance with no false signals.

Table 8.4 conducts a turning point analysis for a variety of forecasts. Four turning points are considered: (1) the beginning of the 1981 recession; (2) the onset of the expansion from that recession in late 1982; (3) the commencement of the 1990 recession; and (4) the recovery starting in the first half of 1991. The specific dates of these turning points in Table 8.4 do not conform to the reference dates given by the NBER Business Cycle Dating Committee. This is because the NBER gives monthly dates and the data for real GDP are quarterly. Moreover, the

Table 8.4

**Forecasts of Real GDP Growth[a]**

| Date of turning point | Actual real GDP growth | UCLA | ML | CB | DRI | WEFA | COMB | ARIMA |
|---|---|---|---|---|---|---|---|---|
| 1981.1 | 5.8 | 0.7 | −1.1 | −1.6 | −0.9 | 0.6 | −0.6 | 5.6 |
| 1981.2 | −1.9 | −0.1 | −2.5 | 1.5 | 0.4 | 0.4 | 0.1 | −2.0 |
| 1982.4 | −2.5 | 0.7 | 2.8 | 1.0 | 2.1 | 2.2 | 1.8 | −0.1 |
| 1983.1 | 3.1 | 3.1 | 4.1 | 4.8 | 2.1 | 4.1 | 3.8 | 0.8 |
| 1990.2 | 1.5 | 3.2 | 2.8 | 3.6 | 3.0 | 3.0 | 3.1 | 3.5 |
| 1990.3 | −0.9 | −3.5 | 1.2 | 1.6 | 0.2 | −1.5 | −0.4 | 3.1 |
| 1991.1 | −2.1 | −2.9 | −1.6 | 0.7 | −2.1 | −0.9 | −1.4 | 0.4 |
| 1991.2 | 2.2 | −2.9 | −2.3 | −1.2 | −2.3 | −0.5 | −1.8 | 0.9 |

*Source*: U.S. Department of Commerce, *Statistical Bulletin, Economic Times,* author's calculations.

[a]For the first two turning points, real GNP data are used for the actual and forecasted data. At that time, the firms did not yet forecast real GDP.

UCLA: UCLA Business Forecasting Project; ML: Merrill Lynch Economics; CB: The Conference Board; DRI: Data Resources/McGraw-Hill, Inc.; WEFA: Wharton Econometric Forecasting Associates; COMB: average of the five forecasts; ARIMA: forecasts obtained from an ARIMA(2,0,2) model.

first column (date of turning point) corresponds with the quarter where real GDP growth actually changed direction in each of the four episodes. This does not correspond perfectly with the NBER reference dates.

In the first quarter of 1981, real GDP grew by 6.5 percent. In the second quarter, real GDP growth became negative. This, then, was the turning point for the 1981 recession. The forecast by UCLA also went from positive (0.7) to negative (−0.1) in those two quarters, so it is credited with having called the turning point. So did Merrill Lynch: Even though that forecast did not change direction, it did go from negative (−1.1) to significantly more negative (−2.5). In a tough call, WEFA is not given credit for signaling the turning point. WEFA's forecast declined from 0.6 to 0.4, but it did not become negative or fall enough in magnitude to be considered a good call. Table 8.5 distills the data in Table 8.4 and states which forecasts were successful in predicting the turning points.

Table 8.5

**Was the Turning Point Forecasted?**

| Turning point | UCLA | ML | CB | DRI | WEFA | COMB | ARIMA |
|---|---|---|---|---|---|---|---|
| Recession of 1981 | Y | Y | N | N | N | N | Y* |
| Expansion beginning in 1982 | Y* | Y | Y | N | Y | Y | Y |
| Recession of 1990 | Y | N | N | Y | Y | Y* | N |
| Expansion of 1991 | N | N | N | N | N | N | N |

Y = yes; N = no; Y* = best performance.

Three of the forecasting establishments had trouble calling the first turning point, the recession of 1981. Since the combination forecast (COMB) is just the average of the five establishment forecasts, it also missed the call. That left the door open for the ARIMA model, which did a remarkably accurate job in predicting the abrupt change in economic growth. But the ARIMA model missed the recession of 1990, while three of the establishments made the call and the other two predicted sluggish growth. (You might notice that a generous scorer gave DRI a "Y" for the 1990 recession. Even though DRI predicted slightly positive GDP growth, it was much lower than its forecast for the previous period.)

Generally speaking, all of the economic forecasting techniques are challenged by turning points in the business cycle. Time-series techniques, such as ARIMA models, seem to have the most difficulty in discerning turning points, particularly recessions. The results for the 1981 recession are unusual in this respect. But even the econometric forecasts have trouble pinpointing the exact dates of changes in the economic environment, though they seem to recognize when a change is imminent.

Some analysts contend that statistical indicators, which we reviewed in chapter 4, are most useful for identifying turning points in advance. This may be true, but it is difficult to tell if the indicators outperform the other techniques. Remember, the indicator approach to forecasting does not result in quantitative forecasts for specific dates.[3] Moreover, the econometric forecasts typically are adjusted with movements in the leading economic indicators in mind.

All in all, the track record of economic forecasts in picking out

Figure 8.1 **In-Sample versus Out-of-Sample Forecasts**

```
              |<-Data used to develop model-->|
Time:  ———————|———————————————————————————————|————————————————————————>
              |<------In-sample forecasts----->|<--Out-of-sample--->
                                                       forecasts
```

turning points in economic activity is not good. The trouble is in identifying the exact date of the business cycle peak or trough in advance. At present, forecasters do well to cite the turning points contemporaneously. Consider the difficulty everyone had in identifying the onset of the 1991 expansion just one quarter in advance. Table 8.5 indicates that no establishment or technique could do it.

## Other Considerations of Forecast Accuracy

### *In-Sample versus Out-of-Sample Forecasts*

The ARIMA model had a hidden advantage in the turning point analysis conducted above. Data from early 1948 to early 1995 were used to estimate the coefficients of the model. Once these were determined, the forecasts reported in Table 8.4 were obtained by pretending it was one quarter before the forecast date and making the prediction just as if we were standing back in that time period. This is known as an "in-sample" forecast. The model was developed with data from 1948 to 1995, and then used to make a "forecast" for the first and second quarters of 1981.

In an out-of-sample forecast, the prediction is made for a period outside of the data set used to develop the model. The forecasts of the five establishments and the combination forecasts in Table 8.4 are out-of-sample. Take WEFA's forecast for the first quarter of 1981: It was made in January 1981 with all the information available up to that point. It probably would be more accurate if WEFA applied its current model to the information available in January 1981. But that would be an in-sample forecast (see Figure 8.1).

This is something to consider when evaluating economic forecasts. Are they in-sample or out-of-sample? In-sample forecasts have an advantage. Imagine that a forecaster develops a new econometric model of the economy. To prove its predictive powers, the forecaster may show what the model would have predicted had it been used over some period of the past. But these are in-sample forecasts and there is no guarantee that the model will perform as well in the unknown future.

### Point versus Interval Forecasts

Another issue to be considered, one that we have ignored completely thus far, is that of interval forecasts. An interval forecast provides a range of values within which the forecast variable is likely to fall. We might say, for instance, that our forecast of real GDP growth for the following year is between 2 percent and 3 percent. This is opposed to a "point" forecast, which provides only a single forecasted value.

Interval forecasts may be developed formally or informally. The formal method involves making a point forecast and forming a one- or two-standard-deviation band around that point. It is not always possible to calculate the standard deviations of forecasts and thus to form a formal interval. ARIMA models and forecasts from regression equations lend themselves to formal interval formation. But any judgmental adjustment of the forecast along the lines discussed in the previous chapter will make it impossible to calculate the standard deviation. As we said then, most economic forecasters adjust their forecasts according to their best judgment. This may explain the predominance of point forecasts in economics.

Informal interval forecasts are just that: The forecaster informally develops a range of values that is likely to encompass the future value of the forecast variable. Most often the forecaster uses experience and judgment to form the range about the point forecast. For example, if the AAE of recent real GDP forecasts is 1.0 percent, a forecaster may feel it is appropriate to form an interval of 2 percent to 3 percent around the point forecast of 2.5 percent. Then again, that range might be widened to 1.8 percent to 3.2 percent if the forecaster believes that economic activity will be especially volatile in the immediate future.

### Revised versus Preliminary Data

Still another consideration to bear in mind when assessing forecast accuracy is whether the forecasts will be compared with preliminary or revised data. At the time a forecast is being developed, the most recent information available is typically preliminary. It will be revised in the months, and years, ahead. When the actual data with which the forecast can be compared become available, they are also preliminary. Should the forecast be compared with the preliminary actual data or should we wait and compare the forecast with the revised data when they become available? If the latter course is chosen, then which revision should be used? GDP data undergo three standard revisions (one month, two months, and one year) after they are released and can be reviewed and amended years later.

For some economic variables it hardly matters which figures are used as the "actual" values with which the forecast will be compared. For instance, a study has shown that forecasts of the change in consumer prices are just as accurate regardless of whether they are compared with preliminary or revised data.[4] Forecasts of GDP, however, appear to be more accurate when compared with the preliminary data.

The decision over which sort of data to use, preliminary or revised, depends on the purpose of the forecasts. Financial markets often respond to the preliminary release of economic statistics and ignore the revisions. Therefore, if the forecasts are to be used to guide financial decisions, then preliminary data should be the benchmark.

Certainly, consistency is important when one is evaluating forecasts. It would be inappropriate to conclude that one set of forecasts is more accurate than another when one has been evaluated in terms of the preliminary data and the other has not.

### Date of Forecast and Forecast Horizon

When evaluating forecasts for accuracy, it is also important to be consistent about when the forecasts were made and for how far in advance. The term "one-quarter-ahead forecasts" means that predictions were made for the next quarter. But this does not specify exactly when the forecasts were made. They could have been made in the last month of the quarter prior to the forecasted quarter. Or they may been made in the first month of the quarter being forecasted, or still later. Since most quarterly data are not available until the end of the first month of the next quarter, forecasts are revised up until that time. Thus, the forecast for a particular quarter may have been made, or revised, after the quarter ended!

Another issue is forecast horizon. Some forecasting techniques are superior for making short-term predictions. Other techniques may have an advantage when the forecast is being made years in advance.

Table 8.6

**The Unemployment Rate: Forecasts and Errors**

| Date | Unemployment rate | Forecast[a] | Error |
|------|------------------|-------------|-------|
| 1989.1 | 5.2 | 5.7 | −0.4 |
| 1989.2 | 5.2 | 5.8 | −0.6 |
| 1989.3 | 5.2 | 5.8 | −0.6 |
| 1989.4 | 5.4 | 5.8 | −0.4 |
| 1990.1 | 5.3 | 5.7 | −0.4 |
| 1990.2 | 5.3 | 5.8 | −0.5 |
| 1990.3 | 5.6 | 5.9 | −0.3 |
| 1990.4 | 6.0 | 5.9 | 0.1 |
| 1991.1 | 6.5 | 5.9 | 0.6 |
| 1991.2 | 6.7 | 5.8 | 0.9 |
| 1991.3 | 6.7 | 5.8 | 0.9 |
| 1991.4 | 7.0 | 5.8 | 1.2 |
| 1992.1 | 7.3 | 5.7 | 1.6 |
| 1992.2 | 7.5 | 5.8 | 1.7 |
| 1992.3 | 7.5 | 5.7 | 1.8 |
| 1992.4 | 7.3 | 5.7 | 1.6 |
| 1993.1 | 7.0 | 5.8 | 1.2 |
| 1993.2 | 6.9 | 5.8 | 1.1 |
| 1993.3 | 6.7 | 5.8 | 0.9 |
| 1993.4 | 6.5 | 5.7 | 0.8 |

*Source*: U.S. Department of Commerce and author's calculations.

[a]The forecasts were developed from a regression where the unemployment rate is explained by the percentage change in real GDP.

Again, consistency is in order. It is improper to compare forecasts that were not made at the same point in time for the same period in the future.

## Autocorrelation

It is important that forecast errors do not display autocorrelation because this would imply that their accuracy could be improved readily. In this context, autocorrelation means that the forecast errors are related, or correlated, with one another. An example will make this clear. Table 8.6 shows quarterly forecasts of the unemployment rate and the errors from those forecasts. Notice the string of negative errors, and then a string of positive errors. Would anyone like to bet that the next error will be negative?

These forecast errors display a classic pattern of autocorrelation.

The error terms are related to each other. When one error is positive, the following error is likely to be positive also. If an error is negative, the next error is likely to be negative. This is not true in every circumstance, but most.

In the example given in Table 8.6, only once is this pattern disturbed. That occurs in the transition from the third quarter of 1990 to the fourth. The error terms switch from negative to positive. But once the error terms become positive they remain so throughout the table. Positive errors reflect overestimates. Do you think that, by the eighth time in a row the forecast overestimated the unemployment rate, the forecaster would have gotten the message and revised the forecast downward? If the forecast errors evince a pattern, that pattern could be exploited to improve forecast accuracy.

The autocorrelation exhibited in Table 8.6 is known as "positive" autocorrelation. An error is expected to have the same sign as its predecessor. There is, however, another possibility—negative autocorrelation. With negative autocorrelation, each error term is expected to have the opposite sign as its predecessor. An overestimate would be followed by an underestimate, which would be followed by another overestimate, and so on. Again, this sort of pattern could be exploited to improve the accuracy of the forecasts.

There are many ways to detect autocorrelation in forecast errors. One approach is make charts of the errors and search for patterns. Figure 8.2 shows charts of the positively correlated error terms from Table 8.6. Figure 8.2a simply plots the errors over time. The clusters of negative, then positive, errors are indicative of positive autocorrelation. Figure 8.2b is a scattergram of the error terms plotted against their previous values. The upward splay of the observations is typical for positively correlated errors.

Negative autocorrelation has its own characteristic patterns. While we will not get into those here, if charts such as these show any pattern, as opposed to a random splay of observations, then autocorrelation is indicated.

Another, more formal, method for detecting autocorrelation among the forecast errors is to calculate their correlation coefficient ($R$).

$$R = \frac{\Sigma(e_t - \overline{e}_t)\,(e_{t-1} - \overline{e}_t)}{\Sigma(e_t - \overline{e}_t)^2}$$

Figure 8.2a **Forecast Errors of the Unemployment Rate**

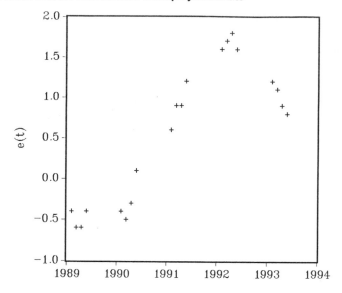

Figure 8.2b **Forecast Errors Plotted against Their Lagged Values**

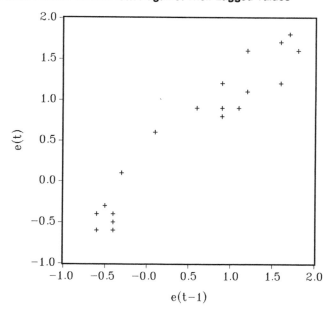

where $R$ is the correlation coefficient of the forecast errors; $e_t$ is the forecast error; $e_{t-1}$ is the forecast error from the previous period; and $\bar{e}_t$ is the average of the forecast errors.

$R$ ranges between $-1$ and $+1$. Extreme values of $R$ indicate the presence of autocorrelation. As a rule, $R$ values greater than 0.7 signify positive autocorrelation while those under $-0.7$ indicate negative autocorrelation. The correlation coefficient ($R$) for the forecast errors in Table 8.6 is 0.94—a severe case of positive autocorrelation.

Autocorrelated forecast errors imply that something is wrong with the forecasting model or procedure. Once again, consider the example in Table 8.6. As the unemployment rate begins to rise in 1990, the forecasts do not rise in tandem. This is what gives rise to the string of underestimates. We have to ask why the forecasts are not picking up on the rise in unemployment. The model must be deficient in some way.

It is possible to exploit the pattern evinced by the forecasts' errors in the presence of autocorrelation to revise and improve the forecasts. However, since autocorrelation implies a deficiency in the forecasting procedure, it is best to get at the root of the problem and correct the procedure or find a more appropriate model.

## Bias

No one wants to have their research or their viewpoint criticized for being biased. The term has a distinctly pejorative flavor. With regard to economic forecasts, the term "bias" has a very specific meaning: The forecast errors, over a very long period of time, should average out to approximately zero. That is to say, over the long haul, the forecasts should neither overestimate nor underestimate the variable being forecasted. Unless a forecast—say, for the unemployment rate in the first quarter of 1990—is perfectly accurate, it will be an over- or an underestimate. One of these does not imply bias. But if a set of forecasts consistently over- or underestimates, then it is said to be biased.

Notice that forecasts can be very inaccurate, yet unbiased. Or vice versa. Similarly, forecasts can be autocorrelated and unbiased or biased. It is best to separate the concepts of accuracy, autocorrelation, and forecast bias in one's mind. Although there are some tenuous relationships among these notions, each is best understood on its own.

### Test Statistic for Bias

The twenty errors of the unemployment forecasts provided in Table 8.6 average to 0.56. Is this close enough to zero for the forecasts to be considered unbiased? A statistical test will answer that question:[5]

*Null hypothesis:* 0.56 is not statistically significantly different from zero—thus, the forecasts are unbiased.
*Alternate hypothesis:* 0.56 is statistically significantly different from zero—thus, the forecasts are biased.

$$\text{test statistic} = \frac{\overline{e_t}}{\sqrt{\Sigma(e_t - \overline{e_t})^2}} = \frac{0.56}{3.74} = 0.15.$$

If 0.15 is greater than the critical value of the test statistic, which is found in a $t$-distribution table, then we will reject the null hypothesis. At the 5 percent critical level, the critical value of the test statistic is 2.093 (there are 19 [= 20 −1] degrees of freedom in this case). Thus, we do not reject the null hypothesis and conclude that the forecasts from Table 8.6 are unbiased.

The main point to understand is that the average forecast error in Table 8.6 was very close to zero and therefore the predictions given there are unbiased. Observe that the forecast errors would not have averaged out to anywhere near zero if we had only considered the errors from the last quarter of 1990 to the end of the table. This time period encompasses only the long string of positive errors. This is why it is critical to have the forecast errors over a long stretch of time when testing for bias. Thirty or more errors are preferred, but as you can see, we made do with twenty in this example.

### Regression Test for Forecast Bias

Another standard test for bias in economic forecasts uses regression analysis.[6] For this test, it is essential that the forecast errors not be autocorrelated. This means we cannot use the unemployment forecasts from Table 8.6. As with the previous test for bias, the more forecast errors there are to work with, the more effectual the test will be.

Table 8.7 gives the rate of inflation as measured by the change in

Table 8.7

**Forecasts of the Change in the Consumer Price Index (Inflation Rate) by the Council of Economic Advisors (CEA)**

| Year | Actual CPI (percent) | CEA forecast (percent) | Forecast error |
|------|------|------|------|
| 1976 | 2.6 | 3.0 | −0.4 |
| 1977 | 3.0 | 2.8 | 0.2 |
| 1978 | 3.0 | 3.1 | −0.1 |
| 1979 | 4.2 | 4.3 | −0.1 |
| 1980 | 5.4 | 4.1 | 1.3 |
| 1981 | 4.8 | 3.8 | 1.0 |
| 1982 | 4.1 | 4.3 | −0.2 |
| 1983 | 3.6 | 3.0 | 0.6 |
| 1984 | 1.9 | 3.5 | −1.6 |
| 1985 | 3.6 | 4.1 | −0.5 |
| 1986 | 4.3 | 4.4 | −0.1 |
| 1987 | 3.2 | 4.9 | −1.7 |
| 1988 | 6.2 | 6.6 | −0.4 |
| 1989 | 10.3 | 12.6 | −2.3 |
| 1990 | 13.5 | 10.7 | 2.8 |
| 1991 | 11.3 | 7.5 | 3.8 |
| 1992 | 7.6 | 6.0 | 1.6 |
| 1993 | 6.5 | 5.5 | 1.0 |
| 1994 | 5.8 | 6.0 | −0.2 |
| AAE | | | 1.0 |
| RASE | | | 1.5 |
| AAPE | | | 19.5 |
| $U$ | | | 0.1 |
| $R$ | | | 0.3 |

*Source: Economic Report of the President,* various issues, and author's calculations.

the consumer price index and the Council of Economic Advisors' (CEA) forecast of that rate. Also shown are the forecast errors. This will make for an interesting example since government forecasts, especially those of the CEA, are often criticized for being consistently overly optimistic—in other words, biased. This example merely updates a portion of a study done by the Federal Reserve Bank of St. Louis.[7]

The four accuracy measures are given as a point of interest. According to the AAE, the CEA's forecasts are typically off by 1 (percent). But there have been some large errors. In 1991, for instance, the forecast vastly underestimated the inflation rate.

The critics claim that the CEA's predictions consistently underestimate the inflation rate because of political pressure on the government to provide a rosy outlook. But the forecast errors in Table 8.7 average out to 0.47, which is close enough to zero to pass the test statistic for bias presented above. Moreover, these forecast errors are not autocorrelated. The correlation coefficient ($R$) is calculated as 0.3, which is well within the prescribed bounds of −0.7 to 0.7.

Since the forecast errors are not autocorrelated, we may apply the regression test for biased forecasts. With this test, the forecasted values are regressed on the actual values. For this specific example:

$$CPI = b1 + b2\ CEAFOR,$$

where *CPI* is the actual inflation rate, and *CEAFOR* is the CEA's forecast.

It can be shown that if the CEA's forecasts are unbiased, then $b1$ will approximately equal zero and $b2$ will approximately equal one. Using ordinary least squares to estimate the regression results in values of $b1 = -0.11$ and $b2 = 1.07$. A formal test shows that these values are not statistically different from zero and one, respectively.[8] These results concur with those from the original study by the Federal Reserve Bank of St. Louis. The critics are wrong: the CEA's forecasts, at least of the inflation rate, are unbiased.

## Ranking the Forecasting Techniques

It is important to remember that it is possible for forecasts to be biased and autocorrelated, yet accurate. But the fact that the forecasts are biased and/or autocorrelated implies that the forecasting model or procedure is in some way flawed. Despite their accuracy, forecasts such as these should be used with the utmost caution.

Also keep in mind the factors that can affect forecast evaluations: (1) Are the forecasts in-sample or out-of-sample? (2) Point or interval forecasts? (3) What are the benchmarks for accuracy—preliminary or revised data? And (4) when were the forecasts made and for what horizon?

With all of this background, we are now in a position to evaluate, compare, and contrast the forecasting techniques presented in the previous chapters. Fortunately, most of the work has already been done elsewhere. Stephen McNees, a researcher at the Federal Reserve Bank in Boston, is the premier authority on the accuracy of economic forecasts. We rely heavily on his research as we rank the forecasting techniques.

Econometric models are the predominant method of forecasting in economics today. In the sections that follow, the forecasting record of each of the alternative techniques is held up to that of the econometric models. A variety of forecasted variables are considered, as are various time horizons. Various combination forecasts are appraised also. May the best technique win!

### Econometric Models versus Naive Forecasts

We have seen already that naive forecasts are not such an easy straw man for more sophisticated forecasts to knock down. Naive forecasts predict that the future value of an economic variable will be what it was for the most recent period. Thus, if real GDP grew by 3.0 percent last quarter, we predict it will grow by 3 percent this quarter.

McNees finds that naive forecasts are more accurate than those generated by econometric models in some instances.[9] He uses the AAE as the accuracy gauge but reports that his results would be no different had other measures been applied. He also reports that his results are invariant with respect to the type of actual data, revised or preliminary, used as the benchmark for accuracy.

Table 8.8 reports the results of an update of McNees's study. It shows the AAEs for four econometric forecasts, the consensus of the econometric forecasts, the naive forecast, and the combination of the econometric and naive forecasts. In case one type of forecast is more accurate in the longer run, both one-quarter-ahead and three-quarter-ahead predictions are considered. The forecasts are quarterly from the third quarter of 1990 to the first quarter of 1995. The forecast errors are determined by subtracting the predictions from the revised actual data.

As confirmation of McNees's findings, there are instances where the naive forecasts are more accurate than those from the econometric models. The naive forecasts of the inflation rate, one quarter ahead, outperform two of the four econometric models. But that situation is not typical. Indeed, all the econometric models and their combined forecasts are more accurate than the naive forecasts of the inflation rate

Table 8.8

**The Accuracy of Econometric versus Naive Forecasts**

| Variable | Average absolute errors (AAE) | | | | | | |
|---|---|---|---|---|---|---|---|
| | UCLA | GSU | DRI | WEFA | COMB1 | NAIVE | COMB2 |
| Growth rate of real GDP | | | | | | | |
| one-quarter-ahead | 1.83 | 1.46 | 1.38 | 1.64 | 1.33 | 1.87 | 1.44 |
| three-quarters-ahead | 1.30 | 1.29 | 1.58 | 1.55 | 1.35 | 2.24 | 1.20 |
| Long-term interest rate | | | | | | | |
| one-quarter-ahead | 0.48 | 0.28 | 0.27 | 0.33 | 0.34 | 0.35 | 0.33 |
| three-quarters-ahead | 0.89 | 0.79 | 0.77 | 0.81 | 0.81 | 0.84 | 0.88 |
| Unemployment rate | | | | | | | |
| one-quarter-ahead | 0.24 | 0.19 | 0.29 | 0.30 | 0.20 | 0.33 | 0.25 |
| three-quarters-ahead | 0.31 | 0.30 | 0.39 | 0.43 | 0.28 | 0.63 | 0.27 |
| Inflation rate | | | | | | | |
| one-quarter-ahead | 1.02 | 1.00 | 0.68 | 0.70 | 0.85 | 0.90 | 0.65 |
| three-quarters-ahead | 0.73 | 0.93 | 0.63 | 0.78 | 0.68 | 1.45 | 0.80 |

*Source:* U.S. Department of Commerce, *Economic Times,* author's calculations.
UCLA: UCLA Business Forecasting Project; GSU: Georgia State Forecasting Center; DRI: Data Resources/McGraw-Hill, Inc.; WEFA: Wharton Econometric Forecasting Associates; COMB1: average of the four econometric forecasts; NAIVE: forecast equals actual value from previous quarter; COMB2: average of the econometric and naive forecasts.

when the forecast horizon is three quarters ahead.

For all four forecasted variables, the performance of the naive forecasts deteriorates dramatically when the forecast horizon is extended beyond one quarter ahead. There is only one instance where the naive forecasts are more accurate than those from an econometric model when the forecast horizon is three quarters ahead. (The naive method beats UCLA's forecasts of the long-term interest rate three quarters ahead.)

The lesson is clear: Naive forecasts are quick and easy to do. They are generated with very little, if any, cost. But you get what you pay for, especially when the forecasts are for more than one period ahead. On the other hand, when the forecasts are for one period ahead, the econometric modelers ought to be ashamed of their slim margin of victory over the naive forecasts.

Before we move on with our competition, there is another point made by McNees and confirmed in Table 8.8: No econometric model dominates the others over all the forecast variables. DRI has the lowest AAE for predictions of the long-term interest rate one quarter ahead. But GSU is the most accurate forecaster of the unemployment rate one quarter in advance. For one-quarter-ahead predictions of real GDP growth, the combination forecasts are more accurate than any of the individual econometric models.

Of course, these rankings can change in the future. But the competent forecast user will be interested to know which forecasters have been the best at predicting which variables over a given time horizon. Skilled forecast users also understand when it is worth paying for an expensive, sophisticated forecast and when a naive prediction will do.

### Econometric Models versus ARIMA Forecasts

Autoregressive integrated moving-average (ARIMA) forecasts were presented in chapter 5. Here we see how these forecasts stack up next to those generated by econometric models. Econometric models are more cumbersome than ARIMA models and more sophisticated. ARIMA models consider nothing except for patterns in the past history of a data series. ARIMA forecasts simply extend these patterns forward given the most recent behavior of the forecast variable. Yet, the patterns that ARIMA models can distinguish are quite complex. As we have seen, ARIMA modeling is well beyond simple trend extrapolation.

Table 8.9 addresses the question of whether ARIMA forecasts are as accurate as those from econometric models. Previous studies indicate that these two forecasting techniques are approximately equally accurate.[10] Table 8.9 replicates Table 8.8 except that the AAEs of ARIMA forecasts are presented instead of those from naive forecasts. For Table 8.9, ARIMA models were developed for each variable separately, using data from the first quarter of 1960 to the second quarter of 1990. Once the ARIMA models were developed, they were used to make out-of-sample forecasts one quarter and three quarters ahead for the third quarter of 1990 through the first quarter of 1995. The AAEs of these ARIMA forecasts are compared with those from the econometric models over the same time frame.

The econometric forecasts of real GDP, both one quarter and three quarters ahead, are more accurate than those from the ARIMA model

Table 8.9

**The Accuracy of Econometric versus ARIMA Forecasts**

| Variable | Average absolute errors (AAE) | | | | | | |
|---|---|---|---|---|---|---|---|
| | UCLA | GSU | DRI | WEFA | COMB1 | ARIMA | COMB2 |
| Growth rate of real GDP | | | | | | | |
| one-quarter-ahead | 1.83 | 1.46 | 1.38 | 1.64 | 1.33 | 1.76 | 1.38 |
| three-quarters-ahead | 1.30 | 1.29 | 1.58 | 1.55 | 1.35 | 1.78 | 1.28 |
| Long-term interest rate | | | | | | | |
| one-quarter-ahead | 0.48 | 0.28 | 0.27 | 0.33 | 0.34 | 0.30 | 0.33 |
| three-quarters-ahead | 0.89 | 0.79 | 0.77 | 0.81 | 0.81 | 0.93 | 0.85 |
| Unemployment rate | | | | | | | |
| one-quarter-ahead | 0.24 | 0.19 | 0.29 | 0.30 | 0.20 | 0.21 | 0.21 |
| three-quarters-ahead | 0.31 | 0.30 | 0.39 | 0.43 | 0.28 | 0.83 | 0.34 |
| Inflation rate | | | | | | | |
| one-quarter-ahead | 1.02 | 1.00 | 0.68 | 0.70 | 0.85 | 0.60 | 0.62 |
| three-quarters-ahead | 0.73 | 0.93 | 0.63 | 0.78 | 0.68 | 1.13 | 0.70 |

*Source:* U.S. Department of Commerce, *Economic Times,* author's calculations.
ARIMA: forecast derived from an ARIMA model; COMB2: average of the econometric and ARIMA forecasts.

in every instance but one. The best forecasts of real GDP three quarters ahead, however, are generated by combining the four econometric forecasts with the ARIMA forecasts. The AAE of this combination (1.28) just beats GSU's forecasts (1.29).

For the long-term interest rate, the ARIMA forecasts are more accurate than three of the econometric models when the forecast horizon is one quarter ahead. But the econometric models assert their superiority at predicting interest rates when the time frame for the forecasts is moved to three quarters ahead.

The same situation holds for the forecasts of the unemployment rate. The ARIMA forecasts are right in the pack, given a one-quarter-ahead time horizon. But the econometric models are obviously superior for predictions made three quarters in advance.

Turning our attention to the predictions of the inflation rate, we see that those of the ARIMA model are the most accurate, again, only for the one-quarter-ahead forecasts. The ARIMA forecasts are least accurate given a three-quarter time horizon.

The figures in Table 8.9 indicate that the ARIMA forecasts can hold their own against the more expensive and unwieldy econometric models only when the forecasts are made for the next quarter. When forecasts are made for three quarters out, the econometric models are far more accurate. Overall, we must conclude that econometric forecasts are superior to those produced by ARIMA techniques. But artful forecasters understand that ARIMA forecasts are very competitive when they are made for the very next quarter. Moreover, it appears as if there can be gains in accuracy by combining econometric and ARIMA forecasts.

### Econometric Models versus Statistical Indicators

It is difficult, if not impossible, to impartially compare the accuracy of forecasts derived from statistical indicators with those from econometric models. Economic indicators offer only qualitative forecasts; they do not give specific numerical predictions. Indeed, the best use of economic indicators may be in identifying impending turning points in the business cycle.

Nevertheless, it was mentioned in chapter 4 that it is possible to form quantitative predictions from statistical indicators such as the leading economic indicators (LEIs) through various means. One of these procedures was referred to as "Renshaw's technique." Another more sophisticated procedure, which is the one we adopt here, employs a regression analysis to derive quantitative forecasts from economic indicators.

The basic idea is quite simple. The statistical indicator is used as the explanatory variable in a regression on the variable to be forecasted. In the following regression, the LEIs are regressed on the growth rate of real GDP:

$$GDP_t = b1 + b2\ LEIs_{t-1} + b3\ LEIs_{t-2} + b4\ LEIs_{t-3} + b5\ LEIs_{t-4} + e_t.$$

The LEIs from the previous four quarters are used to explain changes in the current growth rate of real GDP. Past data on the LEIs and GDP growth will be used to estimate the values of $b1$ through $b5$ as described in chapter 6. This establishes a relationship between previous values of the LEIs and GDP growth. The relationship specified by the regression equation can be used to translate readings of the LEIs

Table 8.10

**The Accuracy of Econometric versus Indicator Forecasts**

| Variable | Average absolute errors (AAE) | | | | | | |
|---|---|---|---|---|---|---|---|
| | UCLA | GSU | DRI | WEFA | COMB1 | INDIC | COMB2 |
| Growth rate of real GDP | | | | | | | |
| one-quarter-ahead | 1.83 | 1.46 | 1.38 | 1.64 | 1.33 | 1.73 | 1.42 |
| three-quarters-ahead | 1.30 | 1.29 | 1.58 | 1.55 | 1.35 | 1.76 | 1.51 |
| Long-term interest rate | | | | | | | |
| one-quarter-ahead | 0.48 | 0.28 | 0.27 | 0.33 | 0.34 | 0.64 | 0.41 |
| three-quarters-ahead | 0.89 | 0.79 | 0.77 | 0.81 | 0.81 | 0.67 | 0.88 |
| Unemployment rate | | | | | | | |
| one-quarter-ahead | 0.24 | 0.19 | 0.29 | 0.30 | 0.20 | 0.64 | 0.42 |
| three-quarters-ahead | 0.31 | 0.30 | 0.39 | 0.43 | 0.28 | 0.62 | 0.57 |
| Inflation rate | | | | | | | |
| one-quarter-ahead | 1.02 | 1.00 | 0.68 | 0.70 | 0.85 | 1.24 | 1.15 |
| three-quarters-ahead | 0.73 | 0.93 | 0.63 | 0.78 | 0.68 | 1.97 | 1.23 |

*Source:* U.S. Department of Commerce, *Economic Times,* author's calculations.
INDIC: forecast derived from an economic indicator; COMB2: average of the econometric and indicator forecasts.

into specific numerical forecasts of GDP growth rates.

Table 8.10 reports the AAEs from indicator forecasts derived by the method described above, and reiterates the AAEs from the econometric forecasts that appeared in Tables 8.8 and 8.9. To obtain the one-quarter-ahead indicator forecasts of real GDP growth, $b1$ through $b5$ of the regression equation above were estimated using data from the first quarter of 1960 to the second quarter of 1990. Then one-step-ahead forecasts were made for each quarter from 1990, third quarter, through 1995, first quarter. The AAE from these nineteen forecasts is reported in Table 8.10: Look under growth rate of real GDP (one-quarter-ahead)—1.73.

To obtain the three-quarter-ahead forecasts, the following regression equation was used:

$$GDP_t = b1 + b2\ LEIs_{t-3} + b3\ LEIs_{t-4} + e_t.$$

It is necessary to drop the first and second lags of the LEIs because these values will not be known when making predictions three periods ahead. Again, data from 1960, first quarter, through 1990, second quarter, were used to estimate $b1$ through $b3$, the structural parameters of the regression. Once these were in hand, past values of the LEIs were used to make three-quarter-ahead forecasts of real GDP growth from the third quarter of 1990 through the first quarter of 1995. The AAE from these nineteen forecasts is reported in Table 8.10 under growth rate of real GDP (three-quarters-ahead)—1.76.

The indicator forecasts of the long-term interest rate and the unemployment rate were obtained in a similar fashion. For the inflation rate forecasts, lagged values of the producers' price index (PPI) were used instead of the LEIs as the explanatory variable. This was done because the LEIs turned out to be very poor predictors of inflation. The PPI worked much better than the LEIs as an indicator of inflation.[11]

The results reported in Table 8.10 demonstrate the superiority of econometric forecasts over those derived from economic indicators. The indicators, however, do win some battles. For instance, when it comes to predicting long-term interest rates three quarters ahead, the indicator forecasts are more accurate than any econometric forecasts or their combination. The only other victory for the indicator procedure comes against the UCLA forecast of real GDP growth one quarter ahead.

Proponents of the indicator approach to forecasting will claim that the comparison shown here is inherently unfair. The procedure for transforming the information embodied in the indicators into exact forecasts, our regression approach, can be criticized. And indicator advocates would rather emphasize the ability of their statistics to identify upcoming turning points in economic activity, as opposed to specific numerical values of given economic variables. And, finally, it should be kept in mind that the econometric forecasts presented here already incorporate, in an informal way, information from economic indicators. Remember that econometric forecasts are always adjusted, often with an eye toward recent movements in the leading indicators.

### Econometric Models versus Vector Autoregressive Forecasts

Vector autoregressions and the forecasts gleaned from them were presented in chapter 6. In this section we gauge the accuracy of predictions that emanate from vector autoregressions (VARs). The Federal Reserve Bank of Minneapolis has been a hotbed of VAR forecasting since the early 1980s.[12] Stephen McNees (1986a) has already compared the forecasts from the VAR model of the Federal Reserve Bank of Minneapolis with those from econometric models. We simply review his study here.

Modern VAR models are as technically sophisticated as econometric models. The statistical techniques deployed in the formation of VARs and in the estimation of their parameters are formidable. But the underlying principle of VARs, which we learned in chapter 6, remains unaltered. That principle is that the relationships among economic variables are far too complex to be captured correctly by any econometric model. Instead of trying to specify these relationships, let us simply assume that everything depends on everything. More specifically, the regression equations of a VAR model explain the behavior of one variable with the past values of all the other variables in the model. Thus, the regression equation for real GDP growth may look like this:

$$GDP_t = b1 + b2\ GDP_{t-1} + b3\ GDP_{t-2} + b4\ UNEM_{t-1} +$$
$$b5\ UNEM_{t-2}\ b6\ UNEM_{t-3} + b7\ INFL_{t-1} + b8\ INT_{t-1} + b9\ INT_{t-2} + e_t,$$

where *GDP* is the growth rate of real GDP; *UNEM* is the unemployment rate; *INFL* is the inflation rate; and *INT* is the interest rate.

In this manner, all the past values of all the macroeconomic variables are used to forecast any given variable. In the regression above, GDP is explained by past values of itself, *UNEM, INFL,* and *INT.* State-of-the-art VAR models have many more variables on the right-hand side of the equation. And state-of-the-art VAR forecasters use imposing methods for determining the number of lags for each variable and for estimating the values of *b*1 through *b*9.[13]

Table 8.11, which is adapted from McNees's study, compares the accuracy of forecasts from the VAR model of the Federal Reserve Bank of Minneapolis with that of three econometric models. Notice that McNees uses the RASE as his accuracy gauge, not the AAE, which we have been using. Another difference is that McNees's study encompasses forecasts made from the second quarter of 1980 through the first quarter of 1985. This gives exactly as many forecasts as we were considering in the previous tables but covers an earlier, and more precarious, forecasting period.[14] McNees's study does not consider forecasts of long-term interest rates. Instead, we substitute the information he provides on short-term interest rates.

Table 8.11

**The Accuracy of Econometric versus Vector Autoregressive Forecasts**

| Variable | Root average squared errors (RASE) | | | | | | |
| --- | --- | --- | --- | --- | --- | --- | --- |
| | UCLA | GSU | DRI | WEFA | COMB1 | VAR | COMB2 |
| Growth rate of real GDP | | | | | | | |
| one-quarter-ahead | n.a. | 3.7 | 4.0 | 4.2 | n.a. | 4.2 | n.a. |
| three-quarters-ahead | n.a. | 2.8 | 3.0 | 3.0 | n.a. | 2.6 | n.a. |
| Short-term interest rate | | | | | | | |
| one-quarter-ahead | n.a. | n.a. | 1.5 | 1.5 | n.a. | 1.6 | n.a. |
| three-quarters-ahead | n.a. | n.a. | 3.0 | 2.8 | n.a. | 3.2 | n.a. |
| Unemployment rate | | | | | | | |
| one-quarter-ahead | n.a. | 0.2 | 0.3 | 0.3 | n.a. | 0.4 | n.a. |
| three-quarters-ahead | n.a. | 0.8 | 0.9 | 1.0 | n.a. | 0.9 | n.a. |
| Inflation rate | | | | | | | |
| one-quarter-ahead | n.a. | 1.9 | 1.6 | 1.7 | n.a. | 2.1 | n.a. |
| three-quarters-ahead | n.a. | 1.7 | 1.4 | 1.7 | n.a. | 2.9 | n.a. |

VAR: forecast derived from a VAR model; COMB2: average of the econometric and indicator forecasts.
*Source:* Adapted from McNees (1986a).

Finally, McNees does not consider any combination forecasts.

Considering the forecasts of real GDP growth, the econometric models are slightly more accurate for one quarter ahead, but the VAR forecasts are significantly better when making predictions three quarters ahead. For the short-term interest rate, the econometric models marginally outperform the VAR models in both forecast horizons. The results are mixed when it comes to the unemployment rate. McNees puts it well when he says that VAR forecasts of the unemployment rate are "among the most accurate." Regarding the inflation rate, however, the econometric models win hands down, especially when it comes to three-quarters-ahead forecasts.

Given these results, it is difficult to declare an overall winner. If, however, econometric models are the reigning forecast champions, then VAR forecasts did not take away their crown in this matchup. In any event, it has been established that VAR forecasts are serious contenders.

*And the Winner Is . . .*

It would defeat the main point we have been attempting to demonstrate throughout the previous sections to proclaim an overall most accurate forecasting technique. That point is that different forecasting techniques are preferable in different circumstances. For instance, given our investigation, econometric models appear to be most accurate when predicting real GDP growth. But when the forecast horizon is three quarters ahead, VAR forecasts are the most accurate. In this category (real GDP growth, three quarters ahead), VAR and econometric models blow the other techniques out of the water. But in another category (the inflation rate, one quarter ahead), ARIMA models and naive forecasts dominate. Understanding this point is one of the keys to using economic forecasts artfully.

Despite the reluctance to rank the forecasting techniques, it is possible to say some things about their relative proficiency. The accuracy comparisons made here support and justify the predominance of econometric models in macroeconomic forecasting today. They do not give the most precise forecasts in every instance, but econometric forecasts are never vastly deficient relative to the other procedures. Another feature of econometric forecasts that bears repeating is that they come with a "story." Econometric forecasters provide not only quantitative predictions, but also the economic analysis that gives rise to them.

Another point to come out of our investigation is that the naive forecasts are not always dreadfully inferior. This fact has implications for the economic forecasting industry. Why all the fuss and expense with these complicated procedures? You cannot do much worse by simply assuming the rate will prevail in the next period. Economic forecasters need to take this criticism to heart. But the fact of the matter is that typically you will do better, and often much better, with state-of-the-art forecasting techniques. This is especially true when the forecast horizon goes beyond the very next period.

Which of the more complex forecasting procedures should be adopted in any given circumstance is a question that requires a crafty forecast user. This chapter has attempted to help the reader with that decision. Keep in mind that the major forecasting establishments rely primarily on econometric models, but they also use the other techniques spelled out in this book. The numerical predictions from the econometric model are then tempered with the results from the other models and procedures.

## Future Prospects

A well-known and well-respected economist once said, "The future is basically unknowable."[15] The statement seems too obvious to be useful. But economists end up saying things like this to remind themselves and anyone who is listening that economic forecasting will never be a perfect science. The future holds unknown shocks to the economy that can never be foreseen and that will foil the most carefully prepared predictions.

One thing is certain: The structure of the economy will change over time. This means old models and perhaps even whole techniques and procedures will have to be revised or scrapped in the effort to keep pace. The real question is: Can the scientific and artful aspects of economic forecasting advance faster than the economy transforms its basic structure? If not, economic forecasting will become less reliable and less useful.

If the past is any guide to the future, economic predictions will become more dependable in the years to come. Economic forecasting has already improved markedly since its modern inception in the 1950s. To illustrate this point, we will unabashedly lift yet another table from a research article by Stephen McNees. Table 8.12 shows the AAEs of forecasts of real GNP growth rates over the decades. The forecasts were made by the Research Seminar in Quantitative Economics (RSQE) at the University of Michigan. RSQE provides the longest string of economic forecasts of any established forecasting outfit and thus allows for a controlled test of forecast accuracy over time. Has the RSQE adapted its forecasting techniques to the changing structure of the economy? The answer is a resounding yes.

Notice the downward trend in RSQE's forecast errors as measured by the AAE. The improvement from 2.1 in the 1950s to 0.9 in the 1980s represents a 133 percent gain in accuracy. It might be claimed that RSQE's forecasting prowess has not improved. The lower AAEs may be the result of the economy becoming easier to forecast. To control for this possibility, McNees also has provided the AAEs from a naive forecast of real GNP growth.[16] If the economy has become easier to predict, then the naive forecast performance should also improve

Table 8.12

**Accuracy of RSQE Forecasts of Real GNP**

| Decade | AAE RSQE | AAE Naive |
|--------|----------|-----------|
| 1950s  | 2.1      | 2.5       |
| 1960s  | 1.0      | 1.4       |
| 1970s  | 1.4      | 3.6       |
| 1980s  | 0.9      | 2.0       |

AAE RSQE: absolute average error of RSQE forecasts; AAE naive: absolute average error of "naive" forecasts.
*Source:* Adapted from McNees (1992, p. 30).

over the decades. It does not. The AAEs of the naive forecasts do indicate that the 1960s were a soft test for economic forecasters, and that may explain why RSQE's forecast performance picks up in that decade. But notice the difficulty the naive forecasts had in the 1970s, while RSQE's forecast errors remained low.

Table 8.12 is forceful evidence that forecast accuracy has improved over time.

## Summary

In the end, the accuracy of economic forecasts must be judged by how useful they are. This is the essence of Theil's statement at the beginning of this chapter. The AAEs for the forecasts of long-term interest rates in Table 8.3 were around 0.3. Is this small enough? Too large? Merely adequate? If these forecasts help investors, traders, and policy makers make better decisions, then they are accurate enough. One assumes that the forecasts do indeed lead to better, more confident decisions, since they are requested and purchased.

On the other hand, AAEs of 0.3 are too large to be useful in some instances. Suppose the Federal Reserve were contemplating an increase in the money supply but had concerns about the effects of this on long-term interest rates. A forecast of those rates with a typical error of 0.3 would be useless to the policy maker deciding between a $15 and $30 billion increase in the money supply. This is because the forecast of long-term rates with a $15 billion increase would be, say, 7.5 percent. If the money supply were increased by $30 billion, the forecast would then be 7.6 percent. The AAE of 0.3 (percent) blurs the two forecasts and does not help the policy maker at the Federal Reserve make a better decision.

The thriving existence of the economic forecasting industry is evidence of the accuracy of economic forecasts. The forecasts must be accurate enough to help with decision making in many situations. Yet there is room for improvement. In fact, more exacting circumstances require more accurate forecasts. If economic forecasts were perfectly accurate, we would depend on them entirely.

## Notes

1. See Theil (1966, pp. 26–39).
2. See McNees (1987).
3. Techniques have been developed to generate date-specific quantitative forecasts from statistical indicators. Renshaw's technique, which we reviewed in chapter 4, is one method for quantifying the forecasts of statistical indicators. See Moore (1969) and Broder and Stekler (1975) for others. Later in this chapter we employ a regression analysis to transform the qualitative predictions of economic indicators into date-specific quantitative forecasts.
4. See McNees (1992).
5. This is a standard $t$-test of the means. More details can be found in any principles of statistics textbook such as Kohler (1988, p. 394).
6. See Mincer (1969) for more details on this regression test for forecast bias.
7. See Belongia (1988).
8. See Gujarati (1992, pp. 404–9) for an exposition of the formal test to determine if $b1$ and $b2$ are statistically different from zero and one, respectively.
9. See McNees (1992, pp. 30–32).
10. See Nelson (1984) and McNees (1992).
11. See Garner (1995) and Moore and Lahiri (1991) for more evidence on the ability of indicators to predict future inflation rates.
12. See Litterman (1986) and Todd (1984).
13. See Webb (1985) for a complete example of a VAR model and an introduction to the statistical techniques used in their estimation.
14. The forecasting period for McNees's study is said to be more precarious because it includes two recessions.
15. The economist was Alan Greenspan, who said this during testimony before Congress as chairman of the Federal Reserve Board in 1994.
16. In this case, the naive forecast is not the simple rule that last period's growth rate will hold in the next period. McNees found this forecast to be terribly inaccurate. The naive forecast in this instance predicts real GNP growth to be its average from the four previous periods.

## References

Belongia, Michael T. 1988. "Are Economic Forecasts by Government Agencies Biased? Accurate?" *Federal Reserve Bank of St. Louis—Review* (November–December): 15–23.

Broder, I., and Stekler, H.O. 1975. "Forecasting with a Deflated Index of Leading Series." *New England Economic Review* (September–October): 15–27.

Garner, Alan C. 1995. "How Useful Are Leading Indicators of Inflation?" *Economic Review—Federal Reserve Bank of Kansas City* (second quarter): 5–18.

Gujarati, Damodar. 1992. *Essentials of Econometrics*. New York: McGraw-Hill.

Kohler, Heinz. 1988. *Statistics for Business and Economics,* 2d ed. Glenview, IL: Scott Foresman.

Litterman, Robert B. 1986. "Forecasting with Bayesian Vector Autoregressions— Five Years of Experience." *Journal of Business and Economic Statistics* (January): 25–38.

McNees, Stephen K. 1986a. "Forecasting Accuracy of Alternative Techniques: A Comparison of U.S. Macroeconomic Forecasts." *Journal of Business and Economic Statistics* (January): 5–15.

———. 1986b. "The Accuracy of Two Forecasting Techniques: Some Evidence and an Interpretation." *New England Economic Review* (March–April): 20–31.

———. 1987. "Forecasting Cyclical Turning Points: The Record in the Past Three Recessions." *New England Economic Review* (March–April): 31–40.

———. 1988. "How Accurate Are Macroeconomic Forecasts?" *New England Economic Review* (July–August): 15–34.

———. 1992. "How Large Are Economic Forecast Errors?" *New England Economic Review* (July–August): 25–42.

Mincer, Jacob, ed. 1969. *Economic Forecasts and Expectations*. New York: Columbia University Press.

Moore, Geoffrey H. 1969. "Forecasting Short-Term Economic Change." *Journal of the American Statistical Association* (March): 1–22.

Moore, Geoffrey H., and Lahiri, Kajal. 1991. *Leading Economic Indicators: New Approaches and Forecasting Records*. New York: Cambridge University Press.

Nelson, Charles R. 1984. "A Benchmark for the Accuracy of Econometric Forecasts of GNP." *Business Economics* (April): 52–58.

Theil, Henri. 1966. *Applied Economic Forecasting*. Amsterdam: North-Holland.

Todd, Richard M. 1984. "Improving Economic Forecasting with Bayesian Vector Autoregression." *Quarterly Review—Federal Reserve Bank of Minneapolis* (Fall): 18–29.

Webb, Roy H. 1985. "Toward More Accurate Forecasts from Vector Autoregressions." *Economic Review—Federal Reserve Bank of Richmond* (July–August): 3–11.

# Bibliography

Anderson, Gerald H. and Erceg, John J. 1989. "Forecasting Turning Points with Leading Indicators." *Economic Commentary—Federal Reserve Bank of Cleveland* (October).

Balke, Nathan S. 1991. "Modeling Trends in Macroeconomic Time Series." *Economic Review—Federal Reserve Bank of Dallas* (May): 19–33.

Balke, Nathan S., and Gordon, Robert J. 1989. "The Estimation of Prewar Gross National Product: Methodology and New Evidence." *Journal of Political Economy* (February): 38–92.

Banks, Jerry, and Carson, John S. 1984. *Discrete-Event System Simulation.* Englewood Cliffs, NJ: Prentice-Hall.

Baumol, William J., and Benhabib, Jess. 1989. "Chaos: Significance, Mechanism, and Economic Applications." *Journal of Economic Perspectives* (Winter): 77–105.

Batra, Ravi. 1987. *The Great Depression of 1990.* New York: Simon and Schuster.

Begg, David K. 1982. *The Rational Expectations Revolution in Macroeconomics: Theories and Evidence.* Baltimore, MD: Johns Hopkins University Press.

Belongia, Michael T. 1988. "Are Economic Forecasts by Government Agencies Biased? Accurate?" *Federal Reserve Bank of St. Louis—Review* (November–December): 15–23.

Bodkin, Ronald G.; Klein, Lawrence R.; and Marwah, Kanta. 1991. *A History of Macroeconometric Model-Building.* Brookfield, VT: Edward Elgar.

Box, G.E.P., and Jenkins, G.M. 1970. *Time Series Analysis: Forecasting and Control.* San Francisco: Holden Day.

Bratt, Elmer C. 1937. *Business Cycles and Forecasting.* Chicago: Business Publications.

Brock, William A. 1986. "Distinguishing Random and Deterministic Systems: Abridged Version." *Journal of Economic Theory*, 40: 168–95.

Brock, W.A., and Sayers, C.L. 1988. "Is the Business Cycle Characterized by Deterministic Chaos?" *Journal of Monetary Economics* (July): 71–90.

Broder, I., and Stekler, H.O. 1975. "Forecasting with a Deflated Index of Leading Series." *New England Economic Review* (September–October): 15–27.

Burns, Arthur F. 1960. "Progress Toward Economic Stability." *American Economic Review* (March): 1–19.

Burns, Arthur F., and Mitchell, Wesley C. 1946. *Measuring Business Cycles.* New York: NBER.

Casti, John L. 1990. *Searching for Certainty.* New York: Morrow.

Chow, Gregory C. 1960. "Tests of Equality between Sets of Coefficients in Two Linear Regressions." *Econometrica* (July): 591–605.

Christ, Carl F. 1975. "Judging the Performance of Econometric Models of the U.S. Economy." *International Economic Review* (February): 54–74.

Christiano, L.; Eichenbaum, M.; and Stock, J. 1990. "Unit Roots in Real GNP:

Do We Know, and Do We Care?; Comment." *Carnegie-Rochester Conference Series on Public Policy*, 32 (Spring): 7–82.

Cole, Rosanne. 1969. "Data Errors and Forecasting Accuracy." In *Economic Forecasts and Expectations*, ed. Jacob Mincer, pp. 47–82. New York: Columbia University Press.

Conference Board. 1966. "The Principle Diffusion Index." *Conference Board Record* (July): 12–14.

Cox, Garfield. 1930. *An Appraisal of American Business Forecasts*, 2d ed. Chicago: University of Chicago Press.

DeJong, David N., and Whiteman, Charles H. 1991. "Reconsidering 'Trends and Random Walks in Macroeconomic Time Series'." *Journal of Monetary Economics*, 28: 221–54.

De Leeuw, Frank. 1991. "Toward a Theory of Leading Indicators." In *Leading Economic Indicators: New Approaches and Forecasting Records*, eds. Geoffrey H. Moore and Kajal Lahiri, pp. 15–56. New York: Cambridge University Press.

Diebold, Francis X., and Rudebusch, Glenn D. 1989. "Scoring the Leading Indicators." *Journal of Business*, 62 (3): 369–91.

———. 1992. "Have Postwar Economic Fluctuations Been Stabilized?" *American Economic Review* (September): 993–1018.

Duesenberry, J.S.; Fromm, G.; and Klein, L.R., eds. 1965. *The Brookings Quarterly Econometric Model of the United States*. Chicago and Amsterdam: Rand McNally and North-Holland.

Eckstein, Otto. 1983. *The DRI Model of the U.S. Economy*. New York: McGraw-Hill.

Epstein, Roy J. 1987. *A History of Econometrics*. Amsterdam: North-Holland.

Evans, Michael K. 1969. *Macroeconomic Activity: Theory, Forecasting, and Control*. New York: Harper and Row.

Fair, Ray C. 1971. *A Short-Run Forecasting Model of the United States Economy*. Lexington: D.C. Heath.

Fels, Rendigs, and Hinshaw, C. Elton. 1968. *Forecasting and Recognizing Business Cycle Turning Points*. New York: Columbia University Press.

Frickey, Edwin. 1942. *Economic Fluctuations in the United States*. New York: Russell and Russell.

Friedman, Milton. 1940. "Review of Business Cycles in the United States." *American Economic Review*, 30: 657–60.

Friedman, Milton, and Heller, Walter W. 1969. *Monetary vs. Fiscal Policy*. New York: W.W. Norton.

Frumkin, Norman. 1990. *Guide to Economic Indicators*. Armonk, NY: M.E. Sharpe.

———. 1992. *Tracking America's Economy*, 2d ed. Armonk, NY: M.E. Sharpe.

Garner, Alan C. 1995. "How Useful Are Leading Indicators of Inflation?" *Economic Review—Federal Reserve Bank of Kansas City* (second quarter): 5–18.

Gleick, James. 1987. *Chaos: Making a New Science*. New York: Viking.

Gordon, Robert J., ed. 1986. *The American Business Cycle*. Chicago: University of Chicago Press.

Granger, C.W.J., and Ramanathan, Ramu. 1984. "Improved Methods of Combining Forecasts." *Journal of Forecasting*, 3: 197–204.

Gujarati, Damodar. 1992. *Essentials of Econometrics*. New York: McGraw-Hill.

Haberler, Gottfried. 1937. *Prosperity and Depression*. Geneva: League of Nations.

Hall, Robert E. 1978. "Stochastic Implications of the Life Cycle–Permanent Income Hypothesis: Theory and Evidence." *Journal of Political Economy*, 86: 971–88.

Hall, Thomas E. 1990. *Business Cycles—The Nature and Causes of Economic Fluctuations*. New York: Praeger.

Henderon, J.W., and Seaman, S.L. 1994. "Predicting Turning Points in Economic Activity with Indexes of Economic Indicators: Improved Reliability Using a Logistic Model." *Business Economics* (January): 40–45.

Hildebrand, George. 1992. *Business Cycle Indicators and Measures*. Chicago: Probus.

Hsieh, David A. 1991. "Chaos and Nonlinear Dynamics: Application to Financial Markets." *Journal of Finance* (December): 1839–77.

Huth, W.L. 1985. "A Quantitative Look at the System of Leading Economic Indicators." *Journal of Macroeconomics* (Spring): 195–210.

Hymans, Saul H. 1973. "On the Use of Leading Indicators to Predict Cyclical Turning Points." *Brookings Papers on Economic Activity*, 2: 339–84.

Juglar, Clement. 1966. *A Brief History of Panics and Their Periodical Occurrence in the United States*. New York: A.M. Kelly.

Keen, H. Jr. 1983. "Leading Economic Indicators Can Be Misleading, Study Shows." *Journal of Business Forecasting*, 2(4): 13–14.

Keynes, John M. 1939. "Professor Tinbergen's Method." *Economic Journal*, 49: 558–68.

———. 1940. "On a Method of Statistical Research: Comments." *Economic Journal*, 50: 154–56.

———. 1973. *The General Theory of Employment, Interest, and Money*. Vol. 7 of *The Collected Writings of John Maynard Keynes*. London: Macmillan.

Kitchin, J. 1923. "Cycles and Trends in Economic Factors." *Review of Economic Statistics*, 5: 10–16.

Klein, Lawrence R. 1964. "A Postwar Quarterly Model: Description and Applications." In *Models of Income Determination*. Vol. 28 of *Studies in Income and Wealth*. Princeton, NJ: Princeton University Press.

Klein, Philip P., and Moore, Geoffrey H. 1991. "Purchasing Management Survey Data: Their Value as Leading Indicators." In *Leading Economic Indicators*, eds. Geoffrey H. Moore and Kajal Lahiri, pp. 403–28. New York: Cambridge University Press.

Kling, James L. 1987. "Predicting the Turning Points of Business and Economic Time Series." *Journal of Business* (April): 201–38.

Kohler, Heinz. 1988. *Statistics for Business and Economics*, 2d ed. Glenview, IL: Scott Foresman.

Kondratieff, Nikolai D. 1935. "The Long Waves in Economic Life." *Review of Economics and Statistics*, 17: 105–15.

———. 1984. *The Long Wave Cycle*. New York: Richardson and Snyder.

Koopmans, Tjalling C. 1947. "Measurement without Theory." *Review of Economics and Statistics* (August): 161–72.

Kuznets, Simon. 1953. *Economic Change*. New York: W.W. Norton.

Litterman, Robert B. 1986. "Forecasting with Bayesian Vector Autoregressions—Five Years of Experience." *Journal of Business and Economic Statistics* (January): 25–38.

Lucas, Robert E. 1981. *Studies in Business Cycle Theory*. Cambridge, MA: MIT Press.

Makridakis, Spyros, et al. 1984. *The Forecasting Accuracy of Major Time-Series Methods*. New York: John Wiley.

Mansfield, E., and Behravesh, N. 1995. *Economics U$A*, 4th ed. New York: W.W. Norton.

McCarthy, Michael D. 1972. *The Wharton Quarterly Econometric Forecasting Model Mark III*. Philadelphia: University of Pennsylvania Press.

McLaughlin, R.L. 1980. "Never, Never-Repeat-NEVER Forecast Recession." *Business Economics* (May): 5–15.

McNees, Stephen K. 1986a. "Forecasting Accuracy of Alternative Techniques: A Comparison of U.S. Macroeconomic Forecasts." *Journal of Business and Economic Statistics* (January): 5–15.

———. 1986b. "The Accuracy of Two Forecasting Techniques: Some Evidence and an Interpretation." *New England Economic Review* (March–April): 20–31.

———. 1987a. "Forecasting Cyclical Turning Points: The Record in the Past Three Recessions." *New England Economic Review* (March–April): 31–40.

———. 1987b. "Consensus Forecasts: Tyranny of the Majority." *New England Economic Review* (November–December): 15–21.

———. 1988. "How Accurate Are Macroeconomic Forecasts?" *New England Economic Review* (July–August): 15–34.

———. 1990. "The Role of Judgment in Macroeconomic Forecasting Accuracy." *International Journal of Forecasting* (October): 287–99.

———. 1992a. "The 90–91 Recession in Historical Perspective." *New England Economic Review* (January–February): 3–22.

———. 1992b. "How Large Are Economic Forecast Errors?" *New England Economic Review* (July–August): 25–42.

Mincer, Jacob, ed. 1969. *Economic Forecasts and Expectations*. New York: Columbia University Press.

Mitchell, W., and Burns, A. 1938. "Statistical Indicators of Cyclical Revivals." In *Business Cycle Indicators*, ed. Geoffrey Moore, pp. 162–83. Princeton, NJ: Princeton University Press, 1961.

Moore, Geoffrey H. 1950. "Statistical Indicators of Cyclical Revivals and Recessions." In *Business Cycle Indicators*, ed. Geoffrey Moore, pp. 184–260. Princeton, NJ: Princeton University Press, 1961.

———. 1969. "Forecasting Short-Term Economic Change." *Journal of the American Statistical Association* (March): 1–22.

———. 1983. *Business Cycles, Inflation, and Forecasting*. Cambridge, MA: Ballinger.

———. 1990. *Leading Indicators for the 1990s*. Homewood, IL: Dow Jones–Irwin.

Moore, Geoffrey H., and Lahiri, Kajal. 1991. *Leading Economic Indicators: New Approaches and Forecasting Records*. New York: Cambridge University Press.

Muth, John F. 1961. "Rational Expectations and the Theory of Price Movements." *Econometrica* (July): 315–35.

Neftci, Salih N. 1982. "Optimal Prediction of Cyclical Downturns." *Journal of Economic Dynamics and Control* (August): 225–41.

Nelson, Charles R. 1972. "The Prediction Performance of the FRB-MIT-Penn Model of the U.S. Economy." *American Economic Review* (December): 902–17.

———. 1984. "A Benchmark for the Accuracy of Econometric Forecasts of GNP." *Business Economics* (April): 52–58.

Nelson, Charles R., and Plosser, Charles I. 1982. "Trends and Random Walks in Macroeconomic Time Series." *Journal of Monetary Economics*, 10: 139–62.

Newbold, Paul, and Bos, Theodore. 1990. *Introductory Business Forecasting.* Cincinnati, OH: South-Western.

Niemira, Michael P. 1991. "An International Application of Neftci's Probability Approach for Signaling Growth Recessions and Recoveries Using Turning Point Indicators." In *Leading Economic Indicators: New Approaches and Forecasting Records*, eds. Geoffrey H. Moore and Kajal Lahiri, pp. 91–108. New York: Cambridge University Press.

Nutter, G. Warren. 1962. *Growth of Industrial Production in the Soviet Union.* Princeton, NJ: Princeton University Press.

Oyen, Duane B. 1991. *Business Fluctuations and Forecasting.* Dearborn, MI: Dearborn Financial.

Palash, C.J., and Radecki, L.J. 1985. "Using Monetary and Financial Variables to Predict Cyclical Downturns." *Federal Reserve Bank of New York Quarterly Review* (Summer): 36–45.

Persons, Warren M. 1931. *Forecasting Business Cycles.* New York: John Wiley.

Persons, W.M.; Foster, W.T.; and Hettinger, A.J. 1924. *The Problem of Business Forecasting.* Boston: Houghton-Mifflin.

Phillips, A.W. 1958. "The Relationship between Unemployment and the Rate of Change of Money Wage Rates in the United Kingdom: 1861–1957." *Economica*, 25: 283–99.

Plosser, Charles I. 1989. "Understanding Real Business Cycles." *Journal of Economic Perspectives* (Summer): 51 77.

Ramsey, James B. 1980. *Economic Forecasting—Models or Markets?* San Francisco: CATO Institute.

Reijnders, Jan. 1990. *Long Waves in Economic Development.* Brookfield, VT: Edward Elgar.

Renshaw, Edward F. 1991. "Using a Consensus of Leading Indicators to Find the Right Ball Park for Real GNP Forecasts." In *Leading Economic Indicators: New Approaches and Forecasting Records*, eds. Geoffrey H. Moore and Kajal Lahiri, pp. 197–209. New York: Cambridge University Press.

Rippe, Richard D. 1992. "Business Economists, Forecasting, and Markets." *Business Economics* (January): 13–20.

Romer, Christina D. 1989. "The Prewar Business Cycle Reconsidered: New Estimates of Gross National Product, 1869–1908." *Journal of Political Economy* (February): 1–37.

Romer, Christina D., and Romer, David H. 1994. "What Ends Recessions?" In *NBER Macroeconomics Annual*, vol. 9, eds. S. Fischer and J. Rottemberg, pp. 13–57. Cambridge, MA: MIT Press.

Rostow, W.W. 1975. "Kondratieff, Schumpeter, and Kuznets: Trend Periods Revisited." *Journal of Economic History*, 35: 719–53.

Samuelson, Paul. 1939. "Interactions between the Multiplier Analysis and the Principle of Acceleration." *Review of Economics and Statistics*, 21: 75–78.

Sargent, Thomas J., and Wallace, Neil. 1975. "Rational Expectations, the Optimal Monetary Instrument, and the Optimal Money Supply Rule." *Journal of Political Economy* (April): 241–57.

Schumpeter, Joseph. 1927. "The Explanation of the Business Cycle." *Economica* (December): 286–311.

———. 1939. *Business Cycles*, vols. 1 & 2. New York: McGraw-Hill.

Sheffrin, Steven M. 1988. "Have Economic Fluctuations Been Dampened? A Look at Evidence outside the United States." *Journal of Monetary Economics* (January): 73–83.

Sims, Christopher A. 1980. "Macroeconomics and Reality." *Econometrica*, 48: 1–48.

Sims, Christopher A., and Uhlig, Harald. 1991. "Understanding Unit Rooters: A Helicopter Tour." *Econometrica* (November): 1591–99.

Sorkin, Alan L. 1988. *Monetary and Fiscal Policy and Business Cycles in the Modern Era*. Lexington, MA: D.C. Heath.

Staller, George. 1958. "Fluctuations in Planned and Free-Market Economies." *American Economic Review* (June): 385–95.

Stekler, H.O. 1991. "Turning Point Predictions, Errors, and Forecasting Procedures." In *Leading Economic Indicators: New Approaches and Forecasting Records*, eds. Geoffrey H. Moore and Kajal Lahiri, pp. 169–81. New York: Cambridge University Press.

Stock, James H., and Watson, Mark W. 1989. "New Indexes of Coincident and Leading Economic Indicators." In *NBER Macroeconomics Annual*, pp. 351–94. Cambridge, MA: MIT Press.

Tainer, Evelina. 1993. *Using Economic Indicators to Improve Investment Analysis*. New York: John Wiley.

Temin, Peter. 1989. *Lessons from the Great Depression*. Cambridge, MA: MIT Press.

Theil, Henri. 1966. *Applied Economic Forecasting*. Amsterdam: North-Holland.

———. 1971. *Principles of Econometrics*. New York: John Wiley.

Tinbergen, Jan. 1968. *Statistical Testing of Business-Cycle Theories*. New York: Agathon Press.

Todd, Richard M. 1984. "Improving Economic Forecasting with Bayesian Vector Autoregression." *Quarterly Review—Federal Reserve Bank of Minneapolis* (Fall): 18–29.

U.S. Bureau of Economic Analysis. 1973. *Long Term Economic Growth 1860–1970*. Washington, DC: U.S. Department of Commerce.

U.S. Department of Commerce. 1984. *Handbook of Cyclical Indicators*. Washington, DC: Government Printing Office.

Valentine, Lloyd M. 1987. *Business Cycles and Forecasting*, 7th ed. Cincinnati, OH: South-Western.

Van Duijn, Jacob J. 1983. *The Long Wave in Economic Life*. London: George Allen and Unwin.

Webb, Roy H. 1985. "Toward More Accurate Forecasts from Vector Autoregressions." *Economic Review—Federal Reserve Bank of Richmond* (July–August): 3–11.

———. 1991. "On Predicting the Stage of the Business Cycle." In *Leading Economic Indicators: New Approaches and Forecasting Records*, eds. Geoffrey H. Moore and Kajal Lahiri, pp. 109–27. New York: Cambridge University Press.

Wecker, W.E. 1979. "Predicting the Turning Points of a Time Series." *Journal of Business* (January): 35–50.

Winkler, Robert L. 1984. "Combining Forecasts." In *The Forecasting Accuracy of Major Time-Series Methods*, Spyros Makridakis, et al., pp. 292–311. New York: John Wiley.

Zarnowitz, Victor. 1984. "The Accuracy of Individual and Group Forecasts from Business Outlook Surveys." *Journal of Forecasting* (January–March): 11–26.

———. 1985. "Recent Work on Business Cycles in Historical Perspective." *Journal of Economic Literature* (June): 523–80.

Zarnowitz, Victor, and Moore, Geoffrey H. 1983. "Sequential Signals of Recession and Recovery." In *Business Cycles, Inflation, and Forecasting*, ed. Geoffrey H. Moore, pp. 23–59. Cambridge, MA: Ballinger.

# Index

# About the Author

**Elia Kacapyr** describes his career in economics as that of a journeyman. Before receiving his Ph.D., he began teaching—first at Georgia State University, where he studied for his doctoral degree, and then at Bloomsburg University of Pennsylvania. From there he was off to Salisbury State University in Maryland and then on to his current position at Ithaca College. Professor Kacapyr primarily teaches econometrics and macroeconomics. He developed and updates the American Trends Index of Well-Being, which is featured each month in *American Demographics* .